THE EDUCATIONAL DECISION-MAKERS

An advanced study in sociology

THE EDUCATIONAL

Aaron V. Cicourel and John I. Kitsuse

University of California, *Northwestern*
Riverside *University*

DECISION-MAKERS

 THE **BOBBS-MERRILL** COMPANY, INC.
A SUBSIDIARY OF HOWARD W. SAMS & CO., INC.
Publishers • INDIANAPOLIS • NEW YORK

Robert McGinnis
CONSULTING EDITOR
Cornell University

74539

ACKNOWLEDGMENTS

The research reported in this volume was begun in 1958 under a grant from the Northwestern University Graduate School Committee on Research Funds. Aaron Cicourel received additional support from the John Randolph Haynes and Dora Haynes Foundation in the form of a summer fellowship. We wish to acknowledge our indebtedness to these organizations.

At various stages of our research, we were most fortunate in receiving invaluable cooperation, skilled assistance, and lively criticism from numerous sources. To the administration and staff of Lakeshore High School and to the students and parents in our sample, we wish to express our special gratitude. During the several months of our field work, they gave generously of their time, energy, and good will as participants in scientific research. We are painfully aware that these words of acknowledgment are wholly inadequate to express our appreciation of their generosity.

We wish also to thank David C. Dietrick and Rose Giallombardo for their excellent research assistance and Mrs. "Bert" Adams for her skillful typing. After careful reading of the manuscript, Harry Singer and Burton R. Clark made many constructive suggestions for which we are most grateful. Finally, we have been particularly fortunate in having the benefit of Robert McGinnis' editorial guidance. The final organization and revision of the manuscript owes much to his pointed criticisms and comments on theoretical and methodological issues as well as on problems of presentation.

CONTENTS

THE EDUCATIONAL DECISION-MAKERS

1. THE SCHOOL AS A

MECHANISM OF SOCIAL DIFFERENTIATION

Among the variety of theoretical and research problems in occupations that interest sociologists is that concerned with the processes by which a population becomes distributed within the occupational structure of the society. Any society must develop techniques for selecting and training its members to fill occupational positions. In modern industrial societies, these techniques have become increasingly specialized and organized within educational institutions.

With the increase in occupational specialization, college training has become the major criterion for stratifying occupations of high and low occupational skill, income, and social prestige. The strategic importance of college training for the occupational distribution of the population has in turn increased the significance of the high school in the structure and process of social stratification, because admission of high school graduates to colleges is often contingent upon their performance in secondary schools.[1] Thus, in their studies of how populations are occupationally differentiated

1 Junior colleges, which have recently increased at a phenomenal rate, particularly in California, provide an alternate route to college admission for students whose high school records disqualify them at the time of graduation for applications for college entrance. The applications for transfer of junior college students, however, are differentially evaluated to their disadvantage, according to a study by Burton R. Clark. (*The Open Door College: A Case Study*. New York: McGraw-Hill, 1960.) See also Leland L. Medsker, *The Junior College: Progress and Prospect*. New York: McGraw-Hill, 1960.

and distributed, sociologists have directed their investigations to the processes of socialization in general, and more particularly to the temporal points within these processes at which the range of occupational aspirations becomes narrowed and focused, choices are made between alternatives, and preparatory activities are begun.

APPROACHES TO THE PROBLEM

The standard approach to the study of students who are and are not admitted to college begins with examination of the characteristics of college-qualified graduates to determine how they differ from those of nonqualified students. The findings of investigations oriented by this approach suggest that the more "obvious" explanations, such as that the college-qualified students have higher I.Q. scores, higher grade records, greater financial support from their parents, etc., than their non-college-qualified peers, are inadequate to account for students who are qualified but do not get to college. For example, a recent volume[2] reports a finding by Stouffer that many students with high I.Q. scores did not go to college. He reports also that of the high I.Q. students who did not go to college, many had consistently good academic records during their high school careers.

In view of such findings, social scientists have increasingly directed their attention to "non-intellective" determinants of educational, occupational, and general life aspirations. Among students whose tested capabilities and course grades are high, the determinants of college-going aspirations and actual college enrollment have been sought in cultural, social, and motivational factors. Performance and achievement are conceived to be products of ability and motivation when talent is above a minimum level considered necessary for success in college. Thus, Turner,[3] using a sample of

[2] David C. McClelland *et al., Talent and Society*. New York: Van Nostrand, 1958. The paper by Samuel A. Stouffer, "Social Mobility of Boys in the Boston Metropolitan Area," delivered at the SSRC Conference on "Non-intellective Determinants of Achievement," Princeton, New Jersey, 1953, is cited on page 16.

[3] Ralph H. Turner, "Reference Groups of Future-Oriented Men," *Social Forces*, 34 (December 1955), pp. 130-136.

male college students, has investigated the motivational significance of the standards of reference groups used by future-oriented students to evaluate the relative success of their own performance. Strodtbeck[4] has also emphasized the social and cultural motivational sources of academic achievement in his study of Jewish and Italian high school students. His findings suggest the motivational significance of group differences in family interaction, particularly power relations in the socialization process and value orientations toward achievement. Similarly, Parsons,[5] Kahl,[6] and others have underlined the importance of social class membership as a major determinant of the occupational aspirations and achievement of youth. They have emphasized class-related differentials in the socialization of children and the consequences of such differences for the attitudes of youth toward academic achievement, occupational aspirations, and plans for college education.

Hollingshead's study of adolescence in Elmtown[7] presents a somewhat different perspective on the relation between social class and the social as well as academic status of students within the school system. His concern with the organization of adolescent activities among the youth in Elmtown directed him to investigate the influences of social class membership upon clique formation and the effects of such cliques upon the treatment and evaluation of students by administrative and teaching personnel within the school. Since the publication of Hollingshead's book, peer groups and related peer cultures and their influences upon the organization of adolescent attitudes, activities, and achievement have been subjects of sociological investigation, both theoretical and empirical.[8] In his recent

4 Fred L. Strodtbeck, "Family Interaction, Values and Achievement," in David C. McClelland *et al.*, *Talent and Society*. New York: Van Nostrand, 1958, pp. 135-191.

5 Talcott Parsons, "General Theory in Sociology," in R. K. Merton *et al.*, *Sociology Today*. New York: Basic Books, 1958, pp. 3-38.

6 Joseph A. Kahl, "Educational and Occupational Aspirations of 'Common Man' Boys," *Harvard Educational Review*, 23 (Summer 1953), pp. 186-203.

7 August B. Hollingshead, *Elmtown's Youth*. New York: Wiley, 1949.

8 See David Riesman *et al.*, *The Lonely Crowd*. New Haven: Yale University Press, 1949, esp. Chapter 3; Carolyn Tryon, "The Adolescent Peer Group," *43rd Yearbook* of the National Society for the Study of Education. Chicago: The University of Chicago Press, 1944, Part I, "Adolescence"; James S. Coleman, *The Adolescent Society*. Glencoe: Free Press, 1961; Talcott Parsons, "Age and Sex in

study, Coleman[9] specifically examined these influences by investigating the normative effects of peer group climates upon the relative valuation of peer achievement in academic, athletic, and social activities among the student populations of ten high schools varying in size and organization.

In the following pages we present an alternative formulation that conceives of the differentiation of students as a consequence of the administrative organization and decisions of personnel in the high school. We shall contend that the distribution of students in such categories as college-qualified and non-college-qualified is to a large extent characteristic of the administrative organization of the high school and therefore can be explained in terms of that organization. We shall be concerned primarily with the relation between the administrative organization of the high school and the ways in which the students are processed through it. More specifically, we wish to investigate how the routine decisions of the guidance and counseling personnel within the high school are related to the college/non-college decisions and, by implication, to the occupational choices made by students.

Our more general concern with the allocation of personnel within the occupational structure of the larger society is similar to that of Parsons. We view as problematic, however, his assumption that the "virtually ascribed" college-going expectation among the middle- and upper-class segments of the population *accounts for* the higher rate of students from those social classes who do in fact go to college.[10] Although he identifies the school and prior academic achievement as the institutional setting within which the college-going expectation is expressed, he does not systematically consider how the formal organization of the school affects the realization of those expectations. In stressing the class-ascribed character of the

---

the Social Structure of the United States," *American Sociological Review,* 7 (October 1942), pp. 604-616; C. W. Gordon, *The Social System of the High School.* Glencoe: Free Press, 1957; Frederick Elkin and William A. Westley, "The Myth of Adolescent Culture," *American Sociological Review,* 20 (December 1955), pp. 680-684.

9 James S. Coleman, *op. cit.;* also "The Adolescent Sub-Culture and Academic Achievement," *American Journal of Sociology,* 65 (January 1960), pp. 337-347.

10 Talcott Parsons, *op. cit.,* p. 27.

college aspiration, he assumes that the organizational processing of the aspiration is routine and non-problematic. We wish to question this assumption in our study.

Although heightened competition for college facilities has stimulated the growth and development of colleges throughout the nation, it has also given impetus to a policy of restricted enrollment for "quality" education and raised the entrance requirements among the "better" colleges to which students of the middle and upper social classes aspire. In view of the changing ratios of supply and demand in college facilities, it should also be noted that the theoretically significant distribution of high school seniors is not the gross college/non-college dichotomy, but the distribution of students according to their admission into colleges ranging from those having the highest applicant/enrollment ratio and admission requirements to those accepting any high school graduate. Class-ascribed college-going expectations might be considered an adequate explanation of the gross college/non-college distribution, but it cannot explain how students are distributed among hierarchically ranked (prestige) colleges. An explanation of such a distribution requires an investigation of the ways in which admission to various colleges is subject to specifically *organizational* contingencies.

Assuming that parents have college aspirations, to whatever quality of college, for their children, and assuming that their children have internalized those aspirations, whether or not such students do in fact became eligible for college entrance depends upon: (1) the communication by parents and/or the student to the school of the student's intention to prepare for college admission; (2) the enrollment of the student in high school courses that will qualify him for college—i.e., courses that will meet college entrance requirements; (3) the satisfactory completion of such courses;[11] and (4), in some instances, the recommendation of high school authorities in support of the student's college applications, particularly in the case of applications to the "better" colleges. Organizational decisions and actions that affect these preconditions may occur at any point

---

11 "Satisfactory" in this context means that the student earned grades that were adequate for admission to the college of his choice.

in the student's transition through the school system and may be quite independent of either his or his parents' aspirations.[12]

In stressing the significance of such organizational contingencies for the explanation of college/non-college or "good"/"better"/ "best" college distributions of the student population, we do not deny that the formal organization of the high school progressively implements the college and occupational goals of the majority of students. Such student goals, however, are processed and actualized through a system subject to the contingencies of organizational processes. Indeed, it is precisely the routine aspects of the organizational processing activity that are of interest and are revealed by the variety of "problems" that attend the movement of a cohort of students through the high school system.

THE CONCEPTUAL FRAMEWORK

In his classic study of suicide,[13] Emile Durkheim underlined the central importance of rates of social phenomena for sociological theory and research. The sociological problem of rates may be stated simply as follows: How are the patterned variations in the rates of certain social phenomena to be accounted for as characteristics, not of individuals, but of the social and cultural organization of the groups, communities, and societies with which they are regularly associated? For example, how is it that rates of juvenile delinquency are higher among Negroes than whites, working-class than middle-class, urban than rural adolescents?

The rates taken to be the "facts to be explained" by sociologists are generally constructed by using statistics compiled and assembled by persons other than sociologists for purposes other than that of scientific research. In establishing the existence of differences

---

[12] The consequences of such organizational activity may be unknown to the student or his parents until he seeks admission to a college, or indeed, they may never become known to him. The articulation of parental and/or student aspirations with the organizational processes that differentiate and channel students through the school system cannot, therefore, be assumed, for it requires a flow of information to, from, and within the family and school organizations.

[13] Emile Durkheim, *Suicide*. Glencoe: Free Press, 1951, pp. 41-53; 297-325.

in the rates of juvenile delinquency among various segments of the population, for example, the sociologist frequently depends upon statistics made available by law-enforcement and other agencies of control. Sociologists generally recognize and acknowledge that such statistics contain errors of under- and over-enumeration that result from the variation between and within agencies of the definitions of categories used in compiling the statistics, the biases of agencies in identifying and processing cases, misclassification of those cases that are identified, etc. The statistics are, nevertheless, used by the sociologist as bases for constructing rates on the justification that, as a practical matter, they are the best available data. A major consequence of such use of agency statistics is that the sociologist, after acknowledging the questionable bases of the rates, assumes the rates as given and proceeds to correlate those rates to various social characteristics—e.g., age, sex, race, family background—of *individuals* who are represented in the rates. This procedure, however, obscures the fact that the variations in the rates that the sociologist seeks to explain are inextricably related to the organizational activities of the agencies that produced the statistics and thus the rates.

In formulating our research, therefore, we proposed to address specifically the problem of investigating the processes by which persons come to be defined, classified, and recorded in the categories of the agency's statistics.[14] If the rates of college-going students, underachievers, "academic problems," etc., are to be viewed sociologically as characteristics of the high school as a complex organization, then the explanation for such rates must be sought in the patterned activities of that organization and not in the behavior of students *per se*. The theoretical significance of student *behavior* for variations in the rates is dependent upon how the personnel of the high school interpret, type, and process that behavior. Thus, the problem was formulated as follows: If the rates of various student types are conceived to be products of the socially organized activities of the personnel, then the question is "How do these activities

14 This view of rates is taken from the work of Harold Garfinkel and can be found in his "Common Sense Knowledge of Social Structures," paper read at the Fourth World Congress of Sociology, Milan, Italy, September, 1959.

result in making a student a statistic in a given category?" Or stated in a more general form: "How are the equivalence classes of given social categories produced?" So stated, our problem was to investigate the day-to-day activities of high school personnel and the conceptions, definitions, and criteria they employed to identify, classify, and record "cases" in the categories of the school's statistics.

The orientation that guided our research application of the problem of rates was drawn from the work of Alfred Schutz[15]—who takes the position that the perspectives of the actors (i.e., the organizational personnel) whose actions produce the ongoing social organization are of central importance for any investigation of how organizations come to define, record, and treat persons as instances of certain social categories. Throughout his work, Schutz underlines the theoretical and methodological principle that the social sciences must deal with social behavior in terms of the *common-sense interpretations of social reality* currently in use by members of the group, organization, or society under investigation. In stressing this principle, Schutz insists that the concepts of the social sciences must be "constructs of the second degree." He states:

> The observational field of the social scientist . . . has a specific meaning and relevance structure for the human beings living, acting and thinking therein. By a series of common-sense constructs they have pre-selected and pre-interpreted this world which they experience as the reality of their daily lives. It is these thought objects of theirs which determine their behavior by motivating it. The thought objects constructed by the social scientist, in order to grasp this social reality, have to be founded upon the thought objects constructed by the common-sense thinking of men, living their daily lives within their social world. Thus, the constructs of the second degree, namely constructs of the constructs made by the actors on the social scene, whose behavior the social scientist has to

[15] The following represent a selection from Schutz's writings: "On Multiple Realities," *Philosophy and Phenomenological Research*, 5 (June 1945), pp. 533-575; "The Problem of Rationality in the Social World," *Economica*, 10 (May 1943), pp. 130-149; "Common-Sense and Scientific Interpretation of Human Action," *Philosophy and Phenomenological Research*, 14 (September 1953), pp. 1-37; "Concept and Theory Formation in the Social Sciences," *The Journal of Philosophy*, 51 (April 1954), pp. 257-273. Harold Garfinkel's paper, "The Rational Properties of Scientific and Common Sense Activities," *Behavioral Science*, 5 (January 1960), pp. 72-83, contains a detailed discussion of the present use of the notion of common-sense interpretations of social reality.

observe and to explain in accordance with the procedural rules of his science.[16]

This theoretical orientation to the study of social organization may be applied to the present problem of explaining the variations in rates of college-going and other student types. Such rates, constructed by the sociologist from the various statistics of the high school, may be conceived as products of the socially organized activities of its personnel. Attention must therefore be directed to those definitions applied and procedures followed by the personnel whereby students are differentiated, labeled, and processed as "college material," "academic problems," "troublemakers," etc. The use of such definitions and their effects upon the interpretations of student behavior by the organizational personnel become the primary source of data for understanding how students come to be classified and distributed among the various categories of the high school's statistics. Schutz states the theoretical importance of these definitions as follows:

> The typifying medium *par excellence* by which socially derived knowledge is transmitted is the vocabulary and syntax of everyday language generalization referring to the relevance system prevailing in the linguistic in-group which found the named thing significant enough to provide a separate term for it. The *pre-scientific* vernacular can be interpreted as a treasure house of readymade pre-constituted types and characteristics, all socially derived and carrying along an open horizon of unexplored content.[17]

Thus, the first research task in our investigation of the rate-producing process was to explore the "vocabulary and syntax" of the language employed by the school personnel to identify the variety of student types recognized as significant in the day-to-day activities of the high school. Such types are the common-sense constructs by which the personnel interpret student behavior and classify them into organizationally provided categories.

The second task was to examine the consequences of these identification and classification processes for the direction and development of any given student's career within the high school. Our use

16 *Op. cit.*, "Concept and Theory Formation. . . ," pp. 266-267.
17 *Op. cit.*, "Common-Sense and Scientific Interpretations. . . ," p. 10. Italics added.

of the term career follows Hughes' suggestive statement that a study of careers "may be expected to reveal the nature and 'working constitution' of a society."[18] As applied to our research, the day-to-day organizational activities of identifying and classifying student types may be conceived to produce a range of careers that lead to different outcomes for students processed through the system. Some careers may qualify students for entrance to accredited colleges and universities and lead to professional occupations. Others may lead to terminal junior college certificates and into the lower ranks of white collar positions, and still others to immediate entrance into the labor market. The concept of career provides us with a method of describing and charting the sequence of the organizational decisions made and actions taken toward students in their movement through the high school system.

In a current study of patient selection in a psychiatric out-patient clinic, Garfinkel and Brickman deal explicitly with the social processes by which a population is differentiated within a social organization. Their study is concerned with "the socially organized and socially controlled ways in which patients and clinic personnel make decisions that decide a patient's transfer from one clinic status to a succeeding one. We wish to study whether and how these ways account for the features of patient load and flow."[19] The design of their study provides us a method of investigating the processes by which different outcomes are produced in an organizational setting. The present formulation follows the framework of their study.

AN OVERVIEW OF THE SUBSTANTIVE ISSUES

In the following chapters we shall direct our attention to how the high school as a socially organized system of activities differentiates talented from average and low-ability students and college-going

18 Everett C. Hughes, "Institutional Office and the Person," *American Journal of Sociology*, 43 (November 1937), pp. 404-413. For another related conception of career, see Erving Goffman, "The Moral Career of the Mental Patient," *Psychiatry*, 22 (May 1959), pp. 123-142.

19 Harold Garfinkel and Harry Brickman, "A Study of the Composition of the Clinic Patient Population of the Outpatient Department of the UCLA Neuropsychiatric Institute," unpublished manuscript, n.d., p. 16.

from non-college-going students, and how such activities may affect the future occupational careers of the student population. We shall not undertake the task of investigating a wide range of phenomena pertaining to student attitudes, values, and behaviors that presumably differentiate the college-going from non-college-going populations. Our interest in these phenomena will be guided by their organizational relevance. That is, the theory of social organization followed here will be applied to decide which of the phenomena are pre-selected and pre-interpreted as significant by the personnel of the high school.

In our study we wish to examine the thesis advanced in earlier studies that social class and organizational sponsorship, as opposed to capability, are critical for the manner in which students are processed through the school system. Since our student sample is drawn from an upper-income community, the students should, consistent with Parsons' hypothesis, be predominantly college-oriented. We seek also to show, however, that the notion of class-ascribed aspirations from which Parsons' hypothesis is derived must be articulated with a conception of organizational processes if we are to understand how effectively those aspirations are implemented for the majority of such students. We hope to shed light on how parental and student knowledge and activity regarding the college-going program influence the organizational processes of the high school.

The theory of social organization that orients our study leads us to conceive of a college-qualified high school senior as the product of the organizational actions of school personnel who record the college/non-college declaration of freshmen students, classify them into ability groups, assign them to types of course programs, review and evaluate their performance, and define, interpret, and counsel them on their problems. We may ask, then: are students with college-going expectations automatically assigned to courses that will qualify them for college entrance at the end of their high school careers? Or, is such assignment subject throughout their high school years to specific organizational contingencies?

The "problems" that are attributed to students by school personnel should not be those which are widely, but generally, discussed as the so-called "adolescent problem." The labels of "underachiever" and "overachiever" and the variety of social and psychological interpretations that are made of them—e.g., "emotionally disturbed," "social isolate," "antisocial"—should be generated by the organizational activities of the school personnel. Our research formulation directs our attention to organizational factors for an explanation of how such students present problems for the high school.

We contend that the organizational production of various student problems is related to the bureaucratization of the counseling system and the professionalization of its personnel. Thus, the organization of the counseling system and the activities of its personnel have been a central focus of our study. Our interviews with counselors were designed to reveal that the clinical orientation of their professional training leads to the fusion of academic problems with personal problems of students. We suggest that among full-time counselors, and particularly among school social workers, the clinical interpretation of academic problems has become a means of explaining deviant cases of students who have capability but who fail to perform at their expected level.

Our study is indirectly tied to the larger question of whether and how the high school in American society operates to provide equal access to higher educational facilities to those of equal capability. The theoretical orientation we follow suggests that one of the major consequences of the current search for academic talent in the high school should be a limitation of access to future occupational opportunities by organizational decisions and actions that occur as early as the students' last year in junior high school. The activities of counseling personnel are of major importance in such organizational decisions and actions and therefore deserve close examination.

ORGANIZATIONAL PROCESSES AND HIGH SCHOOL CAREERS

In the organization of contemporary adolescent life, the high school is the major if not the single formal organizational structure in which the adolescent's achievement in his progress toward adulthood is systematically assessed and recorded. Excluded as he is from equal participation in the social, economic, and political activities of the larger society, the adolescent's school activities provide the major formally organized avenue of achievement that links his present status to his projected adult career. The school, therefore, occupies a strategic position in the organization and control of the adolescent status transition. It serves as a sort of clearing house for other community agencies that come into contact with the adolescent. Thus, the school is the agency to which the police, civic organizations, and welfare agencies, as well as parents, go with their reports, if not complaints, concerning the actual or suspected "problems" of students. The often incomplete records of such communications are filed in the student's cumulative folder. The folder constitutes an official biography reflecting the state of his career at any particular time. As any teacher or counselor would acknowledge, however, a student's career within the school system may also be documented by an unofficial biography that not only supplements the officially recorded information but frequently provides the critically significant interpretation of it. The information, therefore, that is *not* included in the official biography should be an important determinant of the manner in which students are organizationally defined and processed.

Compulsory education, which in most states prescribes school attendance until the age of sixteen, insures the passage of each generation of youth through the school system and an organizational record of their careers within it. The authority and responsibility that are legally delegated to the school are assumed as mandates to "educate the young" in the broad sense of that phrase. Accordingly, the school as an agency of socialization has undertaken the task of developing responsible citizenship and "well-rounded" personalities as well as scholarship among its students. Participation and performance in the school-sponsored and organized extracurricular activities have come to be viewed by school personnel as an important index of the personal, emotional, and social "adjustment" of students.

The recent emphasis on the identification and development of talent in the high school has sharpened the focus of organizational efforts to raise the academic achievement of students. In their implementation of these efforts, the high schools are in many ways thrust into a nation-wide competition for rank and prestige. The criterion of evaluation is productivity, and the gross measure of a school's productivity is the proportion of its seniors who are admitted to colleges. With the increase in production of college-qualified seniors, however, quality as well as quantity has become the standard for judging the excellence of high school programs. The competition for national rank and reputation has been given increasing publicity in recent years, and high schools have sought to maximize their productivity by the application of "scientific" techniques to identify academically talented students and of bureaucratic methods to develop systematically the talent identified.

THE BUREAUCRATIZATION OF THE SEARCH FOR TALENT

The development and application of techniques to identify potentially talented students early in the educational process is one reflection of the increasing specialization of occupational structure in industrial societies. The period of formal educational instruction required to develop potential academic talent into the technical competence required of specialists has extended beyond undergraduate college training to graduate, and in some instances, to postgraduate work. Thus, the investment required in terms of educational facilities and resources has stimulated efforts to increase the efficiency of methods of identifying and recruiting the talented into occupations of critical importance to the society. The current search for academic talent in the high school is the most striking and publicized manifestation of this trend.

A major consequence of the policy of identifying talented students at an early stage in the educational process is that the high school tends to control the students' access to higher educational facilities and, in turn, their life chances. The practice of so-called "ability grouping" is an important structural feature of this control. The assignment of students to ability groups is primarily based on the interpretation of counselors and teaching personnel

of the students' performance on aptitude tests. Since students classified as "low ability" in one or another section of the aptitude tests
are not permitted to enroll in courses required for college entrance,
ability grouping is significantly related to the distribution of educational opportunities among the student population. We wish to
investigate the criteria employed by the school personnel to interpret test results as well as other, less objective measures of student
performance in the processing of students through the system.

Our preliminary field investigations indicated that the counseling
process provided for periodic reviews of student performance as the
major method by which student problems were identified for investigation by counselors. The routinization of this counseling
activity suggests that the academic as well as personal, emotional,
and social "adjustment" of all students will be subjected to examination for evidence of difficulties. As specialists in the identification, interpretation, and treatment of student problems, counselors
would occupy a strategic position in the network of communications
concerning the general demeanor, conduct, association, activities,
and performance of students both in and out of classrooms. Schools
with highly bureaucratized counseling systems, therefore, may be
expected to identify more students with problems.

Preliminary field work also revealed that students with discrepancies between their tested ability and achievement are particularly
subject to counselor attention. Failure to achieve at the expected
level alerts the counselor to investigate the "problem" for indications of "difficulties." An underachiever, for example, may reveal
in a conference with the counselor that he simply failed to submit
his homework in a course ("lacks motivation") or that his mother
always expects him to do better than his brother ("sibling rivalry")
or that he doesn't need any counseling ("reaction against depen-
dency needs"). On the other hand, although students are expected
to achieve up to their ability, evidence that a student has to work
harder than he should for his grades may be considered prejudicial
to his over-all development.

The interpretation of such "problems" in psychological and
clinical terms has important consequences for the degree to which
the policies and methods of the school system remain open to evalu-

ation of their effectiveness and to proposals for modifications. Our counselor interview schedule was constructed to focus investigation on the variety of academic problems that come to their attention. We sought to explore the extent to which some counselors seek explanations by use of a clinical vocabulary that would lead them to interpret those problems in terms of the student's "motivation," "family situation," "peer adjustment," etc.

The presence of social workers in the school we studied prompted us to ask if the failure of the student to respond to psychologically oriented treatment would tend to lead counselors and social workers to look for "deeper problems." We reasoned that, if the student is summoned by the counselor and encouraged to discuss his "difficulty," he may in the face of such solicitous treatment provide information to confirm the clinical interpretation of his "problem." Thus, the organizational efforts to "help" the student may redefine the initial basis of the student's "problem"—i.e., the discrepancy between his capability and classroom performance. One consequence of such an orientation of "help" would be to deflect school administrators from examining the organization and methods of the school system, including the activities of counselors, as sources of academic problems.

Another consequence of this orientation would be the creation of a population of students organizationally differentiated as clinical cases in need of therapeutic treatment. Such a differentiation would presuppose some criteria of normal or healthy adjustment that counselors would presumably apply to identify and interpret problems. We asked, therefore, if there were consensus among school counselors and social workers concerning such criteria. If so, what are the empirical bases for their classifications? We sought also to determine whether and how such interpretations are communicated to the student and to his parents and teachers. When the student is defined as "emotionally disturbed," "anxious," or some similar term by counseling personnel, do the student, his parents, and his teachers accept the clinical labels, or do they propose alternative explanations of the academic problem?

Whether or not they accept the clinical labels, or indeed, even though they may be unaware that imputations concerning the student's "adjustment" have been made, his career within the school system and in later life may be significantly affected by the counselor's judgment. For the counselor's activities involve him in many aspects of the student's life. In addition to the personal counseling discussed above, his duties include vocational guidance, advising students on the programming of courses, certifying them as qualified to participate in extracurricular activities, writing letters of recommendation in support of college and job applications. Thus, we were interested to know when and how the counselor decides that a student with academic problems needs special guidance concerning the college to which he should apply, the occupational careers for which he is most suited, the extracurricular activities in which he should be allowed to participate. To what extent are decisions affected by the counselor's characterization of such students as "insecure," "emotionally unstable," or "aggressive and authoritarian?"

The introduction of clinical terminology and interpretations into the school system is one reflection of the increasing concern in American society for the maintenance of health, particularly mental health. This concern is manifested in virtually all aspects of daily life by such notions as the "emotional maturity" necessary for marriage and parenthood, the "alienative" tendencies of modern life, and the deteriorative effects of the "psychological isolation" of the aged. With the diffusion of such terminology into the vocabulary of everyday life, the individual's status as a "good risk" creditor, employee, scholar, or club member is dependent upon the maintenance of an unmarred reputation as a socially and mentally "well-adjusted" person.

In the context of this increasing stress upon good social and mental adjustment, our study examines the counselor's position of authority and power as a validating agent for the student's future occupational opportunities and careers. Many colleges and employers routinely request unofficial as well as official information in the form of recommendations from school personnel. In many schools such requests presumably would go to counselors as the personnel most intimately informed about the student's high school career. We are interested in knowing what information the counselor recalls about the student and how he recalls it, how these recollections inform his interpretation of the official records, and how the recommendation is phrased. In view of the trend toward the progressive coordination of records and information between the school and other agencies within the society, the student's school career, what is recorded about it, and the counselor's interpretation of it are of more than incidental significance for the processes of social mobility and stratification.

2. THE "ASCRIPTION" OF

PARENTAL AND STUDENT
COLLEGE ASPIRATIONS

In an educational system that is undergoing rapid change, a study of a "typical" high school would be out of date before the findings could be published. Our selection of a school for study, therefore, was not guided by a requirement that it be typical. We looked instead for a school that incorporates the most advanced developments in educational theory and practice. We selected a large, comprehensive high school, hereafter called "Lakeshore High School," with a national reputation for the excellence of its educational program and its student products.

How is Lakeshore High School atypical? First, there is considerable pressure for students to go to college, particularly to the "good" or "prestige" colleges and universities. The pressure is general as well as specific and is exerted by parents, peers, and school personnel. Further, at Lakeshore High, administrative decisions are crucial for the process by which students are qualified for college entrance. These decisions may be independent of the students' college-going aspirations, and they significantly control the flow of students through the several curricula of the high school. Such pressures and administrative decisions do not exist or are of minimal importance in most contemporary high schools, especially in those states where state colleges and universities automatically admit students on completion of a high school program of academic courses. In states where junior colleges exist there is virtually no barrier of any kind, since admission is not contingent upon administrative decisions or completion of an academic program, but on minimal test and course grade requirements.

What can be learned by studying an atypical high school like Lakeshore High? First, there are many high schools of its kind throughout the United States, located in the suburban areas of metropolitan regions and in the wealthier or middle- and upper-middle-class sections of large cities. Second, most American high schools have similar bureaucratic structures and organizational practices, so that the kinds of decisions that are routinely made about students at Lakeshore High are likely to appear with increasing frequency in schools throughout the country. The differentiation of students described in this book probably resembles that found in less "advanced" high schools, but the decisions (and the criteria employed in making them) that produce the differentiation are more important at Lakeshore High because of the strong emphasis placed not only upon going to college but upon attending one of a select group of "good" colleges.

The most important reason for studying this high school is that it has a highly developed counseling system and a curriculum notable for its range and quality. At Lakeshore High the program, procedures, and services have been patterned explicitly on the recommendations presented in the White House Conference "Goals for Guidance."[1] The student-counselor ratio runs from 100 to 1 to 250

[1] The "Goals for Guidance," (Washington, D.C.: U. S. Government Printing Office, 1960) of the 1960 White House Conference of Children and Youth recommended:

"That guidance and counseling programs be strengthened, expanded, and coordinated at all levels; and that the role of the guidance and counseling program be clearly defined. That guidance and counseling begin in the elementary school with educational and vocational planning based on early, continuous, and expanded testing and diagnostic appraisal of each child in order to identify abilities, weaknesses and problems, mental, physical, and emotional.

"That school resources for identification and guidance of the gifted, limited, and otherwise exceptional child, as well as for the average and normal youth, be expanded and improved. That the qualified professional staff (of every school system) include educational and vocational guidance counselors, job placement counselors, physical health personnel, psychologists to assist in diagnosis and continued study of the children, and school social workers or visiting teachers to assist in the treatment of children with special problems.

"That the number of students per counselor in secondary schools be decreased from the present ratio of 625 to 1, to 250 to 1."

to 1, with the average case load 225 to 1. The program for ability-grouped classes at Lakeshore High and its counseling system (which includes social workers, psychiatrists, psychologists, and other specialists at all levels of the school system) reflect the general concern to differentiate students academically and to prepare them for college. Thus, although Lakeshore High is atypical among contemporary high schools, its curricular organization, administrative policies, and counseling system are likely to be adopted and developed more widely within the American school system. An understanding of the organizational practices and decisions whereby students are differentiated is important *per se,* but it is also likely that our study of an atypical high school can provide a preview of the future.[2]

THE SOCIAL CHARACTERISTICS OF LAKESHORE HIGH SCHOOL

Lakeshore High School is located in a high-income suburb of a large metropolitan region. The 1960 Census reports show that the median income for local families was $9193 and the median educational level was 13.5 years for males and 12.6 for females. The occupations reported were in high proportion professional (24%), managerial (19%), and clerical and sales (26%). In the large city of which the community served by Lakeshore High is a suburb, median income for families is $7342, median education is 10.9 years for males and 10.8 years for females, and the occupational distributions shows 11% professional, 11% managerial, and 17% clerical and sales.

The percentage of Lakeshore High graduates who go on to col-

[2] A final comment is in order here on the limitations of our study. Our initial research design called for a simple comparison of two high schools: one with a small college-going population where administrative decisions were not crucial and where the counseling system was undeveloped, and a second school similar to the one chosen for this study. Our failure to carry out the initial objectives stemmed from the unfortunate but nevertheless real problems of inadequate time and resources. Finally, we have not sought to test any hypotheses in this study but to explore the utility of an organizational framework for examining the mobility routes that one part of the educational system provides.

lege is high—from 70 to 75.[3] The Lakeshore college representative is sent periodically to colleges that are especially popular with its students. This enables the high school to maintain good relations with such colleges and to remain in close contact with the latest changes in admissions policies. It is not unusual for some colleges to call the high school when unexpected openings occur in their freshman classes.

Of the Lakeshore class of 1959, 73.25 per cent (N = 649) went to college. Although there have been some minor fluctuations, there have not been any major changes in the past five years in the percentage of college-attending seniors or in the geographic distribution of the colleges they have attended. Roughly 80 per cent have gone to midwestern schools and 15 per cent to eastern schools, while the remaining 5 per cent have gone to southern and western colleges.

THE ORGANIZATIONAL CHARACTERISTICS OF LAKESHORE HIGH SCHOOL

Lakeshore High School currently enrolls approximately 3,600 students and employs about 200 administrative and academic personnel, excluding clerks and stenographers.[4] The general organization consists of four divisions with an equal number of students. Each division is headed by a division principal and three division assistants. The division principals report directly to the superintendent, but they handle all activities within their divisions. The superintendent delegates authority to both the assistant superintendent (who also is called the assistant principal because the superinten-

[3] The college representative at Lakeshore High is in touch with representatives of various colleges, including the so-called "prestige" colleges in the East. Each year representatives from a wide variety of colleges visit Lakeshore High to interview students personally. The high school urges students to contact alumni of colleges that interest them and maintains for this purpose a list of such alumni in the metropolitan area.

[4] Lakeshore High is, by current educational standards, rather large. Its bureaucratic character, therefore, is probably enhanced by sheer scale.

dent is the principal as well as superintendent of the entire high school) and the administrative assistant. Division principals and other administrative officials are often instructed to channel their problems through the administrative assistant.

Within each division there are four counselors, a social worker, and three homerooms, which are managed by division assistants. There is at least one counselor for each grade level in the division (freshman, sophomore, junior, and senior), while the social worker covers the entire division. The counselors and social workers report directly to the division principal, but they are also responsible, respectively, to the heads of the counseling group and of the social workers. These latter two officials report directly to the superintendent and his assistants. Finally, there are various department chairmen, such as those for business, art, combined studies (a combination of English and social studies), English, home economics, foreign languages, and the like, which cross-cut the four divisions. The division structure, then, is primarily an administrative device for handling a large student population under a decentralized system.

The students coming into the high school are randomly assigned to the four divisions, with some noteworthy exceptions. The first exception is that high-ability students are separated and distributed equally among the four divisions. This amounts to a planned separation along administrative lines. It is not clear why the randomizing procedure used for assigning all students would not accomplish the same objective for high-ability students. The second exception is the separation of Negro students and their equal distribution among the four divisions. Again, it is not clear why the randomizing device is not used. It appears that this administration has been concerned with an unknown amount of Negro-white dating. The subject is a touchy one around the high school and we were discouraged from asking questions about it.

The Curriculums. The basic division of curriculums within the school is that between college and non-college courses. The students visit the school while in the eighth grade, take a battery of tests, and are asked to consider a choice between two plans—of which one prepares them for college and the other does not. All freshmen are required to take an English and history course (either as two separate courses or as a combined course from the same instructor), a mathematics course (either basic mathematics, general mathematics, or algebra), a course in freshman arts (art, home economics, industrial arts, music, or speech), and a course in physical education. Variations of this basic program of courses will be explained below.

The students are told to consult their parents and to declare their choices at a later visit to the high school during the same spring semester prior to matriculation. The choice of courses does not reside entirely in the hands of parents and students. The choice of mathematics, for example, is based in part upon the student's performance on one or more tests and upon the junior high school teacher's appraisal of the student. Only students who have achieved a certain level on the tests and/or who have been recommended by their junior high school teachers are advised to enroll in algebra. The general mathematics course is more elementary than algebra and is for students "who have a history of weakness and lack of achievement in arithmetic and reading."[5] The only course that carries college entrance credit is the one in algebra.

The science course may be either general science or laboratory science. Qualified students are allowed to choose between science and a foreign language. The laboratory science course for freshmen is by invitation of the science department only and carries college entrance credit, while the general science course does not.

It should be clear that there are three possible college entrance credit courses that can be taken by the student in his freshman year: algebra, laboratory science, and a foreign language. Of the three algebra is the most critical; if the student does not take it in the freshman year, it becomes increasingly difficult to complete the college-required mathematics sequence because of the other graduation requirements that must be fulfilled. In general, if the student does not take any of the three college preparatory courses, then it will be difficult for him to fit them into his later programs. This is

---

[5] The Lakeshore High Student Manual.

particularly true for students seeking entrance to prestige colleges that recommend a large number of advanced high school courses.

REMARKS ON THE RESEARCH DESIGN

In our research we decided to focus upon three groups: a student sample of approximately 100; the parents of the students in the sample; and a group of 22 counselors (including several part-time counselors). Our interview schedules, which were standard but different for each of the samples, were mostly open-ended. The questions were designed to pinpoint the social processes whereby students and parents made decisions on the choice of curriculum and future aspirations, their knowledge of the curriculum, and their interaction with the school. The counselors were interviewed to investigate how students are differentiated by various official and unofficial criteria. The social workers were also interviewed to determine how further differentiation of students occurred.

One of the four divisions was chosen arbitrarily, and a sample was drawn from the incoming freshman class during the spring semester prior to their entrance to the high school. The parents were approached by mail and telephone for appointments and interviewed the summer before their children became high school freshmen. The students, counselors, and social workers were interviewed during the freshman year (1959-60). Details of general methodological procedures may be found in the appendix.)

Originally the student sample consisted of 105 students, but before we could even communicate with the parents it became apparent that we would lose a few cases. Seven were lost when families moved out of the school district. In addition, we were unable to interview 9 parents and 5 students of the remaining 98 in the sample. We attempted to arrange interviews by phone with the 9 parents, and after several unsuccessful calls we considered them inaccessible. Of the 5 students we were unable to interview, one was classified by the school as an educable mentally handicapped student. This student's parent, however, was interviewed. The remaining 4 students were scheduled for interviews several times, but when they repeatedly failed to appear for the interview, which was conducted in an office at the high school, they were dropped from the sample.[6]

THE "ASCRIPTION" OF COLLEGE-GOING EXPECTATIONS

Parsons has hypothesized that the college-going expectation is a virtually ascribed characteristic among students from middle- and upper-class families.[7] The socioeconomic background of our student sample is reflected in the strong college-going orientation of the entire sample (see Table 2.1) in their formal declaration of choice

Table 2.1   College Intention as Declared by Students in Junior High School

SOCIAL CLASS	COLLEGE	NON-COLLEGE	N
Upper three	70	3	73
Lower two	8	6	14
N	78	9	87*

* Two students did not declare choice.

between the college and non-college curriculums. Our materials appear to support the general hypothesis discussed by Parsons. To

[6] Of the 9 parents not interviewed, 7 refused to be interviewed. The children of 4 of these parents did not plan to go to college, according to their school records; the children of 3 indicated their intention to go to college. The children of the 2 remaining parent refusals were interviewed, and both stated their intention to go to college. Our materials do not permit us to say much more about the interview refusals except to state that there was an apparent lack of interest in our research on the part of those parents whose children were not planning to go to college.

[7] Talcott Parsons, "General Theory in Sociology," in R. K. Merton *et al., Sociology Today.* New York: Basic Books, 1958. To obtain a social-class distribution of our sample, we used Hollingshead's two-factor (education and occupation) index. (*Two Factor Index of Social Position,* privately printed.) We obtained information on education and occupation for 89 parents, and the Hollingshead procedure produced 16 in Class I, 23 in Class II, 36 in Class III, 8 in Class IV, and 6 in Class V. The distribution is consistent with the census characteristics for the community and provides evidence that Lakeshore serves a high socioeconomic clientele. Our reference to social class is designed to call attention to the high socioeconomic status of the school studied; class is not being used as a significant independent variable. The Hollingshead index shows that 75 of the 89 (84 per cent) of the sample for whom we had data fall into the upper three classes.

explore the notion that it is the social and cultural environment of family life that leads to the ascriptive character of college-going expectations, we asked the parents in our sample the following questions:[8]

> What do you think your child would like to do after leaving high school? (If the parent did not mention college plans, the following question was asked:)
> Does your child plan to go to college?

The responses to these questions are presented in Table 2.2. The

Table 2.2   Parental Declaration of Child's College Intention

SOCIAL CLASS	COLLEGE INTENTION			
	YES	NO	DON'T KNOW	N
Upper three	73	1	1	75
Lower two	6	1	7	14
N	79	2	8	89

table reveals that 97 per cent (73 out of 75) of the parents from the upper three social classes stated that their children intend to go to college. These responses lend further support to the ascription hypothesis.

One implication of the ascription hypothesis is that going to college is so routinely assumed among middle- and upper-class parents and children that college plans are made with little if any question that the children will in fact go to college. To explore this implication, we questioned the parents as follows:

> Do you remember the first time that the subject of college was discussed? (This question was asked of only those parents who stated their children were planning to go to college.)
> How old was your child then?
> Has there ever been any question about whether your child would go to college?

The questions were asked so as to permit parents to reveal how and in what contexts college plans were discussed. We hoped to

---

[8] The coding of the questions asked of our subjects may be found in the appendix, where examples are given for each question.

obtain statements that would indicate whether or not the college-going expectation had ever been considered problematic or seriously questioned. Indeed, many parents spontaneously responded that they had "always taken it for granted." The questions were coded to classify responses by whether first discussion of college occurred when the child was in elementary or in the junior high school. This dichotomous classification was constructed on the assumption that discussion of college plans during the earlier (i.e., elementary school) period may be interpreted as strong indication of the ascribed character of the college-going expectation.

Our materials suggest that for parents of the upper three classes there is no question that their children will go to college. Table 2.3 shows that 79 per cent (59 out of 74) indicated that there was no

Table 2.3   Earliest Discussion of College by Whether There Was Any Question of Going

SOCIAL CLASS	COLLEGE DISCUSSED IN ELEMENTARY SCHOOL		COLLEGE DISCUSSED IN JR. HIGH SCHOOL		
	GOING PROBLEMATIC*	GOING TAKEN FOR GRANTED	GOING PROBLEMATIC*	GOING TAKEN FOR GRANTED	N
Upper three	12	52	3	7	74
Lower two	2	3	5	0	10
N	14	55	8	7	84†

* (Finances, grades, or lack of interest.)

† Five parents (1 from the upper three classes with a mentally retarded child and 4 from the lower two classes) did not mention college as a possibility after high school.

question and that many of them—56 per cent of the 59 parents—spontaneously indicated that they have "always taken it for granted."[9] Our interview material, then, supports the ascription hypothesis.

An unstated implication of the ascription hypothesis is that the

[9] Although we have too few cases to speak seriously about the lower two classes, it may be of passing interest to note that it was more characteristic of parents of these two classes to state that for various reasons—financial difficulties, the student's poor grades, his lack of interest—they have considered the possibility that their children may *not* go to college. For most of these parents there was no discussion of college until the child entered junior high school.

college-going expectations among the middle and upper social classes is independent of the student's ability—i.e., that college-going expectation is determined by social class rather than ability. To illustrate this implication of the hypothesis, we contrasted the parents' college expectation with their children's capability as it is measured by the Scholastic and College Aptitude Test (SCAT) administered by the high school to incoming freshmen.[10] The independence of the college-going expectation and tested ability is indicated in the statements of parents whose children have SCAT scores in the 50th percentile or lower categories. (See Table 2.4a.) Thirty-five

Table 2.4a   Distribution of Parent College Declaration by SCAT Scores

| SCAT SCORES | COLLEGE YES | | COLLEGE NO OR UNCERTAIN | | |
	UPPER THREE CLASSES	LOWER TWO CLASSES	UPPER THREE CLASSES	LOWER TWO CLASSES	N
76-100	28	0	0	0	28
51-75	21	2	0	0	23
26-50	12	2	0	3	17
0-25	11	3	1	3	18
N	72	7	1	6	86*

* Three cases had no SCAT scores: 2 from upper three classes, 1 from lower two.

students, of whom 24 are from the upper three social classes, have SCAT scores in the 50th percentile or lower categories. Of these 24, all parents, with one exception, stated that they expect their children to go to college. Parents of students with SCAT scores above the 50th percentile stated without exception that their children intend to go to college. (Among the Class IV and Class V parents, 5 of the 11 whose children have SCAT scores in the 50th percentile or lower categories stated that their children plan to go to college.)

The students' declaration of college-going intentions examined

10 Hereafter, references to student capabilities are to SCAT scores unless otherwise specified.

with reference to their SCAT scores is similar to that of their parents, although there are six discrepancies. (See Table 2.4b.) Most of the students from the upper three classes (18 out of the 20 for whom we had information) with SCAT scores in the 50th percentile or lower categories declared their intention to go to college. (Among the Class IV and Class V students, 6 out of the 11 in the 0 to 50 SCAT categories declared such an intention.) The ascribed character of the college-going expectation among the three upper classes is clearly reflected in our illustrative materials.

Table 2.4b   Distribution of Student College Declaration by SCAT Scores

| | COLLEGE YES | | COLLEGE NO OR UNCERTAIN | | |
SCAT SCORES	UPPER THREE CLASSES	LOWER TWO CLASSES	UPPER THREE CLASSES	LOWER TWO CLASSES	N
76-100	27	0	0	0	27
51-75	21	2	0	0	23
26-50	10	4	0	1	15
0-25	8	2	2	4	16
N	66	8	2	5	81*

* Three cases had no SCAT scores: 2 from upper three classes, 1 from lower two. Five students were not interviewed.

Another way to explore the ascription hypothesis is to compare the student's junior high school grade-point average with his and his parent's statements concerning college-going intentions. Tables 2.5a and 2.5b clearly indicate the independence of college declara-

Table 2.5a   Distribution of Parent College Declaration by Eighth-Grade Point Average

| | COLLEGE YES | | COLLEGE NO OR UNCERTAIN | | |
GRADE-POINT AVERAGE	UPPER THREE CLASSES	LOWER TWO CLASSES	UPPER THREE CLASSES	LOWER TWO CLASSES	N
1.00-1.50	16	0	0	0	16
1.75-2.00	17	1	0	0	18
2.25-3.00	20	2	0	1	23
3.25-4.00	8	3	1	5	17
N	61	6	1	6	74*

* No grade points given for 15 cases: 13 from upper three classes, 2 from lower two.

Table 2.5b   Distribution of Student College Declaration by Eighth-Grade Point Average

GRADE-POINT AVERAGE	COLLEGE YES		COLLEGE NO OR UNCERTAIN		
	UPPER THREE CLASSES	LOWER TWO CLASSES	UPPER THREE CLASSES	LOWER TWO CLASSES	N
1.00-1.50	16	0	0	0	16
1.75-2.00	17	1	0	0	18
2.25-3.00	17	2	1	1	21
3.25-4.00	5	5	1	3	14
N	55	8	2	4	69*

* No grade points given for 15 cases: 13 from upper three classes, 2 from lower two. Five students not interviewed.

tion and grade-point average.[11] Where grade-point average was below *B,* all but one of the parents from the three upper social classes (28 out of 29) and all but 2 of the students (22 out of 24) declared college-going intentions. (The lower two social classes, although the number is small, show a similar tendency, especially the students.)

Our materials are intended to illustrate that among the middle and upper social classes, parents routinely expect their children to go to college, and their children consistently reflect such expectations. The college-going expectation persists independent of whether the student's tested capability is high or low and irrespective of his prior school performance as recorded in his grades. But our interest here is in how the college-going expectation is expressed by parents and students in activities that would implement the student's educational goal, and how such activities are articulated with the school's activities in differentiating college-going from non-college-going students.

PARENTAL PARTICIPATION IN COLLEGE-GOING ACTIVITIES

As we have stated in Chapter 1, neither the aspirations of parents to send their children to college nor the student's formal declaration of college-going intentions (whether or not such aspirations and

[11] Averages were computed for the students' eighth grade marks with the following weightings: $1.00 = A$, $2.00 = B$, $3.00 = C$, and $4.00 = D$.

declarations are ascribed) automatically produces a college-qualified student at the end of his high school career. Whatever the parent's aspirations, a student must, first of all, have fulfilled some minimum college entrance requirements during the course of his high school studies. This contingency is an obvious one, but it is not one which can be met merely by "orientation toward college" or even superior performance in the classroom. With the increased competition for college entrance, the student's high school program must be planned carefully in order to complete the required as well as the recommended courses for college entrance. Furthermore, changes in entrance requirements made by college admissions offices may render a student's plans to enter a particular college obsolete by his senior year in high school. Thus, the process of becoming a college-qualified student may require not only the long-range planning of a program of courses, but also obtaining specific and detailed information concerning college requirements.

Information concerning such requirements may be obtained by parents of Lakeshore High students from a variety of sources: the orientation meeting organized by the high school for parents of incoming freshman students; literature distributed by the high school and a variety of books and pamphlets published to advise parents about how to prepare their children for college; information that may be obtained from friends, neighbors, and relatives who are presumed, on whatever basis, to be informed. Finally, college-educated parents may draw upon their own past experience and knowledge as a basis for advising their children.[12]

Our interest, then, is in ascertaining the kinds of knowledge parents have about college entrance requirements, the sources of such knowledge, and whether and how it is used by parents in advising their children in the planning of the freshman course programs. An exploration of the ascription hypothesis requires that we go beyond finding out that parents of middle- and upper-class students in our study "take it for granted" that their children will go to college. We wish to consider two interpretations of the ascription

12 Knowledge about such requirements may be unimportant in some sections of the country where junior colleges or colleges with nonselective admissions policies but high tuition admit students regardless of poor grades and low test scores.

notion. On the one hand, the hypothesis may be interpreted as implying that the college orientation of such parents is systematically directed to facilitating the progress of their children toward their educational goal. Therefore, these parents should actively engage in activities that will provide them with the most complete information concerning the means of qualifying their children for college. An alternate interpretation more consistent with our theoretical perspective would be that the college-going expectation is so "taken for granted" that middle- and upper-class parents do not consider it problematic that their children will fulfill the college entrance requirements as a "matter of course."

Knowledge of college requirements. In exploring the alternate interpretation, we sought questions that would make problematic the extent to which college-oriented parents have specific and detailed knowledge about college requirements. Thus, if parents "take it for granted" that their children will go to college, such knowledge would be considered to be "what everybody knows"; and when they are asked specific but open-ended questions about college requirements, their information would be general if not vague. Such parents may be expected to express the common-sense conception that if a student plans to go to college, and if his family is able to send him, the high school may be expected as a matter of course to prepare him to gain admission to college. The diffuse common-sense conceptions of parents concerning the requirements for college entrance may minimize the recognition by parents of contingencies that may impede or effectively deflect students from the progressive implementation of their educational goals.

In questioning parents concerning their knowledge of college requirements, therefore, it is important that the questions do not present the respondents with the very knowledge that is being investigated. If parents were presented with forced choices between specific items about college requirements (e.g., four years of English, two years of a foreign language; two years of mathematics, etc.), the form of the questions would obscure the common-sense character of parental responses regarding entrance requirements. The social distribution of knowledge documented by such a method would attribute to parents a greater knowledge and awareness of the importance of the organizational processes of the high school for college admission than may in fact be the case.

We asked parents the following question:

> What sorts of requirements does he (she) have to meet for college entrance?

Before we present the responses of parents to this question, we should note that entrance requirements vary from college to college. In this sense, "it depends" is an appropriate response to the question. The college preparatory curriculum at Lakeshore High School, however, is designed to qualify students for the "best" colleges—i.e., those which recommend or require a substantial surplus of academic courses—as well as for colleges with less selective admissions policies. It is not necessary, of course, for students to take the full complement of courses offered at Lakeshore High to qualify for admission. Furthermore, the organization of the curriculum emphasizes the importance of the sequence in which the courses are taken during the four-year high school period. We shall discuss the importance of the sequence of courses in the next chapter.

Table 2.6 presents the distribution of knowledge among parents as indicated by their responses to the above question concerning

Table 2.6   Parental Knowledge of College Requirements by Whether College Is Taken for Granted

KNOWLEDGE TYPES*	COLLEGE TAKEN FOR GRANTED		COLLEGE NOT TAKEN FOR GRANTED		
	UPPER THREE CLASSES	LOWER TWO CLASSES	UPPER THREE CLASSES	LOWER TWO CLASSES	N
I	9	0	5	1	15
II	5	0	16	1	22
III	18	3	19	1	41
N	32	3	40	3	78†

* Type I refers to an exact specification of each requirement, i.e., foreign language, mathematics (algebra and geometry), laboratory science, history or social studies, and English.

Type II refers to a mention of one or two of the mathematics, science, and language requirements.

Type III indicates a complete lack of knowledge of requirements.

† No response to this question by one subject. Ten parents of non-college-directed students were not asked this question.

college entrance requirements. The responses were classified with reference to the organization of the college-preparatory curriculum at Lakeshore High School. Our materials suggest that information about college requirements is very general and that parents are not aware of the importance of the organizational processes which affect the students' progressive accumulation of college entrance credits. Parents who take college-going for granted are no more knowledgeable about college requirements than those parents who simply state that their children intend to go to college.

Active seeking of information. If the parents' knowledge about college entrance requirements were more or less vague and general, did they seek specific and detailed information about them? The parent orientation meeting sponsored by the high school presented parents with an opportunity to obtain such information. All parents of incoming freshman students were notified and invited by letter to attend the meeting at which the organization of the curriculums, procedures of registration and course assignments, college entrance requirements, etc., are discussed by members of the school personnel. Inasmuch as the orientation meeting represented an officially sponsored occasion for obtaining information, we wished to ascertain whether or not the parents attended the meeting as an expression of their college orientation, whatever information they may or may not have gained from them.

Our parent sample was asked the following question:

Did you attend the meeting at Lakeshore High School held for parents of entering freshmen last February?

Table 2.7 shows the number of parents who attended the meeting. There are no striking differences in the attendance of parents

Table 2.7 Parental Attendance at School Meeting by College Intention and Whether Going to College Is Taken for Granted

SOCIAL CLASS	COLLEGE TAKEN FOR GRANTED		COLLEGE NOT TAKEN FOR GRANTED		
	ATTENDED	DID NOT ATTEND	ATTENDED	DID NOT ATTEND	N
Upper three	17	16	27	13	73
Lower two	2	1	0	3	6
N	19	17	27	16	79*

* Of the 10 non-college cases, 2 attended the meeting.

in these several categories, although apparently a larger number of parents who do not take college for granted attended the meeting (27 or 62 per cent as opposed to 19 or 52 per cent for the "take college for granted" group). The responses to this question suggest that a strong parental college orientation is not expressed in this form of information-seeking activity.

Other questions included in our interview schedule to explore the parents' college-going activity concerned whether they had talked to others about college requirements; if so, with whom they had discussed the subject; and what the content of the discussion was. These questions were designed to probe the common-sense character of the parents' college orientation. Parental responses to this set of interview questions are presented in Table 2.8, which shows

Table 2.8   Parental Discussion about College with Others by Whether or Not College Is Taken for Granted

	COLLEGE REQUIREMENTS DISCUSSED				
	COLLEGE TAKEN FOR GRANTED		COLLEGE NOT TAKEN FOR GRANTED		
SOCIAL CLASS	YES	NO	YES	NO	N
Upper three	8	24	12	28	72*
Lower two	1	2	1	2	6
N	9	26	13	30	78†

* One parent did not respond.

† None of the 10 parents of the non-college group sought information from others regarding college requirements.

that fewer than half of the entire college-expected group (22 out of 78 or 28 per cent) discussed college requirements with others. Whether or not the parents took college for granted appears to make little difference in their participation in this form of information-seeking activity.

The vague character of the college orientation among parents is further evident when we examine the statements made by parents who stated they had discussed college requirements with others. Four talked to the high school counselor—two of these talked about college requirements in general terms, while two asked about the requirements that must be met for specific colleges. A fifth parent visited the college to which the family intended to send their child, and two parents reported they casually discussed the subject with relatives and friends. In general the statements of parents indicate that inquiries concerning college requirements were made rather casually and unsystematically, and for the most part they were directed toward persons "who might know something about it," e.g., one of the child's former teachers, a relative who had attended or was now attending a college, a neighbor who was an alumnus of a college, or, as one parent said, "somebody over at the high school." The most striking features of these comments are their vagueness (even when the responses were probed for more specific details) and the little that was remembered about the discussions they reported. (Examples of these responses may be found in the appendix on coding.)

Participation in program planning. Finally, we questioned parents concerning their participation in planning their children's freshman program of courses. Our questions again attempted to probe the parents' college orientation and the common-sense character of this interest. We asked:

> Have you had anything to do with planning your child's high school program? (If the answer was yes, we asked:)
> In what way?

We expected these questions to tell us which parents were most active in planning their children's first-year high school program and whether such activity was directed toward insuring that the student enrolled in college-preparatory courses. Concern and discussion about college credit courses should be distinguished from the relatively minor decisions that students and parents are asked to make regarding the freshman course program, such as whether to take English and history in a combined course or as separate courses, or to elect speech arts rather than chorus or technical arts, etc.

The responses to these questions are presented in Table 2.9,

Table 2.9   Parent Recommends One or More Courses to Student in Planning Freshman Program

SOCIAL CLASS	RECOMMENDED COLLEGE COURSES*	RECOMMENDED NON-COLLEGE COURSES	N
Upper three	23	12	35
Lower two	2	4	6
N	25	16	41†

* Either language, mathematics, or science.

† Forty-eight parents did not participate in helping their children plan their freshman program.

which illustrates the point that less than half the parents report they participated in the planning of their children's freshman program (41 out of 89, or 46 per cent). In the upper three classes 23 out of 35 (or 66 per cent) mentioned courses relevant to college entrance requirements. But the responses of parents to these questions indicate that of the most strongly college-oriented parents (i.e., those from the upper three classes), 23 out of the 75, or 31 per cent, of the college-declared parents are not active in helping their children plan for courses most relevant for the implementation of college-going plans.

With reference to the ascription hypothesis, the parental responses to the several questions presented in this section underline the importance of investigating how the college-going expectation is interpreted and expressed from the actor's point of view; in this instance, from that of the parent. Parents who have no knowledge whatever of the courses their children must take in high school to meet college entrance requirements may nevertheless state that a college education is "taken for granted." Thus, the ascribed expectation may be quite independent of any activity of parents' vis-à-vis the organizational processes of the high school to insure that the child will in fact be qualified for college at the end of his high school career. A corollary of this statement is that no greater knowledge about college requirements or about the significance of the organizational processes of the high school may be attributed to parents of students who as seniors are college-qualified than to parents of students who are not. The ways in which the college-going expectations of parents and students of the middle and upper classes are articulated with the organizational processes to implement those aspirations are what we find of particular interest in our parent interviews.

STUDENT ORIENTATIONS TOWARD COLLEGE

We turn now to our student interview materials to examine how the college orientation of parents is reflected in the statements of their children, and how the college-going intention is implemented in an organizationally defined choice. Table 2.1 has shown that *most* of the students in our sample are recorded by the school as having declared an intention to go to college. This declaration is made by junior high school students as prospective high school freshmen, in the form of a choice between the college and non-college preparatory curriculums. In the orientation literature distributed to the students and parents and in the official briefings presented by the admissions personnel of Lakeshore High School, these curriculums are called Plan I and Plan II, College-Preparatory and Non-College Preparatory respectively.

In questioning the students about the choice they made during their last semester in junior high school, we referred to the curriculums by the official labels to probe the student's common-sense knowledge of the school's organizational procedures and vocabulary. We were interested in his knowledge of the two plans as a reflection of what he interpreted the choice between them to mean when he was required to make his declaration, and what they meant to him at the time of the interview, i.e., as a freshman in high school. The students were asked the following questions:

> I see that you had to choose between Plan I and Plan II. What plan did you choose? (If the student did not know the difference between the two plans, he was told what they meant.)
> Does it make any difference what plan you choose?
> How do you mean?

The responses, which are presented in Table 2.10, show that of

Table 2.10   Student Knowledge of Difference Between Plan I (College) and Plan II (Non-college) and Choice Made

SOCIAL CLASS	STUDENT KNOWS DIFFERENCE BETWEEN PLANS AND CHOOSES		STUDENT DOES NOT KNOW DIFFERENCE BETWEEN PLANS AND CHOOSES		
	PLAN I	PLAN II	PLAN I	PLAN II	N
Upper three	26	0	42	0	68
Lower two	4	1	4	4	13
N	30	1	46	4	81*

* Two cases were not recorded because they did not know the difference between plans and did not know if they would go on to college (upper three classes).

One case was not recorded because the student did not know the difference between plans and did not know if her interest in nursing required that she go to college (lower two classes).

Five students were not interviewed (upper three classes).

the 76 who were officially recorded as having chosen Plan I, 30 were able to distinguish between the two plans and 46 were not. The students from the upper three social classes were largely ignorant of the differences between the two plans between which they were required to choose in junior high school. The organizationally required declaration seems to have been made without a clear knowledge of the official categories in terms of which the choice was made. This suggests that the act of declaring the choice was presented to them by the school personnel in more simplified terms, such as "Do you plan to go to college?"

We note, however, that the student's declaration of choice was not necessarily a direct reflection of his parents' statement regarding his college-going plans. There are six cases in which the parents' statements do not agree with their children's declaration. Five of these are cases in which the parents plan to send their children to college but those plans are not consistent with the students' choice of the non-college (Plan II) curriculum. In the sixth case, the parent stated that the child would not go to college but the student declared his choice of Plan I. An examination of these deviant cases reveals that discrepancies between the parent's statement and the student's declaration occur when the parent insists that his child intends to go to college regardless of poor grades, evidence of low ability (as indicated by test results), and lack of interest. Although our data clearly show that in the great majority of cases the college orientation of parents is faithfully reflected in the organizational declaration of their children, the official recording of the choice can nevertheless be problematic when the student, through error or intention, reverses parental plans by his choice of a curriculum.

We turn now to the question of the student's choice of a curriculum and his interest in and knowledge about the implementation of the educational goals implied by the choice. The students were asked the following questions:

What sorts of entrance requirements do you have to meet to get into college?
Have you talked to anyone about college requirements?
With whom did you talk?
What did he (she, they) tell you?

The students' responses to these questions, which were also asked of parents in similar but not identical form, are presented in Table 2.11. Less than half (27 out of 66 for 41 per cent) the students

Table 2.11   College-requirement Knowledge of College-oriented Students, by Discussion with Family, School, or Friends

	KNOWLEDGE TYPES*								
	DISCUSSED REQUIREMENTS WITH OTHERS				DID NOT DISCUSS REQUIREMENTS WITH OTHERS				
SOCIAL CLASS	I	II	III	IV	I	II	III	IV	N
Upper three	9	9	5	4	9	9	5	16	66
Lower two	0	1	0	2	2	0	0	1	7
N	9	10	5	6	10	9	6	17	73†

* Type I refers to knowledge of science, mathematics, and language.
  Type II refers to knowledge of mathematics and language, *or* mathematics and science, *or* language and science.
  Type III refers to knowledge of mathematics *or* language *or* science.
  Type IV refers to a "don't know" response, or when the student did not mention any of the three requirements.
  † No response to the question for 1 Class IV student. No interview with 1 Class I and 3 Class III students.

in the upper three classes who chose the college curriculum discussed college requirements with others; those who did discussed them primarily with their parents. Like the statements made by their parents about college requirements, virtually all the reports by students concerning such discussions are vague and quite general. Our materials suggest that in general students in the upper three classes are not informed about the substance or the importance of meeting college requirements. Over-all, our student interview materials present a picture of students who are definitely college-oriented but do not have specific information or concern about the courses they must take to implement their educational goals.

We have examined several implications of the ascription hypothesis with our materials concerning the students' and parents' information-seeking activities and knowledge of the high school curriculums and college entrance requirements. These materials suggest the limitations of the hypothesis. Our next task is to explore the organizational differentiation of students and the ways in which organizational processes articulate the college aspirations of our sample. The question is: How is the actualization of the college orientation of middle- and upper-class parents and students to be explained if their knowledge and activities do not appear to be important elements in implementing college goals?

3. THE ORGANIZATIONAL

DIFFERENTIATION OF INCOMING FRESHMEN

In this chapter we explore how the students in our sample are organizationally differentiated and processed by the admissions personnel of the high school. The general question we wish to address is: How are the college-going intentions of our students articulated with the organizational processes of the high school? In addressing this question, we shift our attention to the activities of the school personnel that structure and validate the movement of students toward or away from their stated goals and aspirations.

THE COLLEGE-GOING DECLARATION

In principle, the student is entitled to exercise his right to choose either the college or non-college curriculum independent of his capability, past performance, or personal and social characteristics, and the high school is committed to honor his choice by providing the conditions for the implementation of his educational goal. In practice, however, the student's declaration of choice is not the only criterion of differentiation employed by the admissions personnel. The manner in which a student is processed as a "college-going" student is contingent not only upon those attributes that in principle he may consider irrelevant—i.e., the above-mentioned capability, past performance, etc.—but also upon interpretations of those attributes by admissions personnel. Thus, a study of the distribution of college- and non-college-going high school seniors that attends only to the individual's goals and the strategies he uses to achieve them does not reveal how the actualization of those goals is contingent upon the perceptions, decisions, and actions of the school personnel.

The first indication of how the student's declaration of college-going intention is translated into organizational terms may be seen in the student's freshman program of courses. The question may be asked: Are students who have chosen the college curriculum in fact enrolled in college-preparatory courses? Before we examine our materials with reference to this question, several features of the curriculums at Lakeshore High School should be noted.

First, most of the courses in the freshman program are prescribed for all students—English, history, mathematics, science, or a foreign language, an elective (which may be chosen from such courses as speech, chorus, mechanical drawing, or home economics), and physical education. Second, the freshman college-preparatory curriculum is distinguished from the non-college curriculum by the *types* of mathematics and science courses included in the program and by the foreign language course. Three mathematics courses are offered: algebra, general mathematics, and basic mathematics. Of the three, algebra, a prerequisite for courses in higher mathematics, is the only college entrance course. General mathematics does not carry college entrance credit, but it does prepare the student for algebra. Basic mathematics is a course designed for students with low mathematical aptitude. Two types of science courses are open to freshmen—biology, which is classified as a laboratory science and thus carries college entrance credit, and general science, which does not. In the freshman year, the student may elect a foreign language instead of a science, thus working toward fulfilling the foreign language requirement for college entrance.

A third feature of the curriculums at Lakeshore High School is that enrollment in algebra, biology, and foreign language is not by the student's election alone. His election of the courses is reviewed by the admissions personnel, who may or may not approve his election. That is, the enrollment of a student in those courses which differentiate college preparatory from non-college courses is by *assignment* based on the admissions personnel's assessment of his capability and performance. The formal criteria applied to assess capability will be discussed below. The point we wish to make here is that meeting college entrance requirements as a freshman is contingent upon the student's choice of the proper courses *and* his assignment to those courses by the admissions personnel.

Assignment to courses. The alternative combinations of courses that can be assigned may be classified as college-preparatory (i.e., includes two college entrance credit courses), quasi-college-preparatory (includes one college credit course), and non-college (includes no college credit courses) programs. We shall refer to the three combinations of courses as Type A, Type B, and Type C programs respectively. Table 3.1 presents the distribution of students who

Table 3.1   Assignment of College-declared Students to Types of Programs

SOCIAL CLASS	COURSE TYPE			
	A	B	C	N
Upper three	48	16	6	70
Lower two	2	3	3	8
N	50	19	9	78

have declared college-going intentions among the three types of course programs. Of the 78 students who formally declared college-going intentions by their choice of Plan I, the majority (50 out of 78 or 64 per cent) were enrolled in Type A, while 28 (36 per cent) were placed in Types B and C. While assignment to Type B does not necessarily mean that the student will not eventually complete a college preparatory program, it does substantially lower the possibility of that outcome, and thus it represents a partial discrepancy between the formal declaration of college-going intentions and assignment to a college course program.

How is this discrepancy between the students' formal declaration of college-going intentions and their assignment to the three types of programs to be accounted for? If the distribution of students among the three types of programs is not a matter of election but rather of assignment, and if capability is the primary criterion of assignment, then we should expect a systematic relation between the students' SCAT scores and the types of programs to which they are assigned. Table 3.2 shows that 9 of the upper three social class

Table 3.2   Types of Programs* Assigned to College-declared Students by SCAT Scores

SCAT SCORE	UPPER THREE CLASSES			LOWER TWO CLASSES			
	TYPE A	TYPE B	TYPE C	TYPE A	TYPE B	TYPE C	N
76-100	25	1	0	0	0	0	26
51-75	14	7	0	1	1	0	23
26-50	8	2	2	1	1	0	14
0-25	1	3	4	0	1	2	11
N	48	13	6	2	3	2	74†

* See p. 51 for definitions of types.
† No information on 4 students.

students with SCAT scores between 0 and 50 are assigned to the Type A program, while 8 such students in SCAT categories 51 to 100 are assigned to Type B programs. This suggests that the assignment of a student to a program is not based solely on the declaration of college-going intention and a SCAT score within a given range.

If the SCAT score is not the primary criterion for distributing students among the types of programs, it might be suggested that actual performance as indicated by the students' past course grades might better account for the distribution. It might be argued that admissions personnel would be more strongly guided by past performance than by a single index of academic potential, of which the SCAT is presumably a measure. As a measure of past performance, we have computed a grade-point average from the students' course grades for their last semester in junior high school.[1] Table 3.3

[1] Only mathematics, social studies, general science, and English were considered. Letter grade *A* was scored one point, while letter grade *F* was scored five points. A simple average was computed.

Table 3.3 Types of Programs* Assigned to College-declared Students by Eighth-grade Point Average

GRADE-POINT AVERAGE	UPPER THREE CLASSES			LOWER TWO CLASSES			
	TYPE A	TYPE B	TYPE C	TYPE A	TYPE B	TYPE C	N
1.00-1.50	7	1	0	0	0	0	8
1.75-2.00	11	2	0	0	0	0	13
2.25-3.00	17	5	0	2	1	1	26
3.25-4.00	11	6	2	0	2	1	22
4.25-5.00	1	0	4	0	0	0	5
N	47	14	6	2	3	2	74†

* See p. 51 for definitions of types.
†No information on 4 students.

presents the grade-point averages of college-declared students assigned to types of programs. If we arbitrarily take the 2.00 grade-point average or higher (i.e., *B* or better) as the cutting point for the assignment of students to the Type A program, the tables shows that from the upper three social classes 63 per cent (29 out of 46) of the students with grade-point averages below *B* are assigned to Type A programs and 37 per cent (17 students) assigned to Types B (11) and C (6).

In view of the discrepancies that result when we apply the SCAT and grade-point criteria to account for the assignment of students to types of course programs, it appears that other, unknown judgments enter into the decisions by which the assignments are made and that the implementation of the student's declaration of college-going intention is far from a matter of course. Whatever the criteria of assignment to types of programs may be, the student's educational plans are subject to this organizational contingency at the very outset of his high school career.

Honors and opportunity courses. The student's college-going plans are affected by a second set of organizational decisions concerning his freshman course program. These decisions are related to the practice of "ability grouping" that is a feature of the Lakeshore High School curriculum. The school curriculum provides courses for students of three broad capability categories: honors courses for those with consistently high performance on tests and/or course grades; regular courses for students classified as "low-average, average, and slightly better than average"; and "opportunity" courses for students with consistently low performance on tests and course grades. Students are classified into ability groups on the basis of their SCAT and STEP scores.[2]

In assigning students to the ability-grouped sections of the various courses, the chairman of each department is authorized to interpret the student's capability and to place him in the appropriate section. In this assignment process, the student's past performance in junior high school and the recommendations of his eighth-grade teachers as well as his SCAT and STEP scores are reviewed. Two levels of honors sections are provided for the best students—advanced honors and honors—in English, history, mathematics, science, and foreign language. Students are invited to enroll in the advanced honors courses, an invitation which they or their parents may decline. Enrollment in honors courses, on the other hand, is by assignment and is not optional. Students with poor records may be assigned to the "opportunity" sections of any or all of the courses in their program.

Several organizational features of ability grouping are specifically relevant for the assignment of freshmen to the three types of course programs discussed previously. First, biology is open to freshmen as an honors or advanced honors course; there are no "regular" or "opportunity" sections of this course. A second feature of the ability-grouping procedure is that there are no "opportunity" sections of algebra or foreign languages. Thus, students who are considered to have low ability are automatically excluded from those courses which differentiate the college from non-college course programs. The exclusion of students who have declared college-going intentions from enrollment in college credit courses depends

<hr/>

[2] The reader will note that in the following discussion no reference is made to STEP (Sequential Test of Educational Progress) scores. We examined such scores in relation to assignments of students to types of course programs and to ability groups which is discussed below. The STEP scores add little to the discussion of the organizational differentiation of students.

heavily upon the department chairman's judgment of the students' capabilities and the importance he assigns to the reliability and validity of the records and other information on which his judgment is based.

A third organizational feature to be noted about the ability-grouping practice is that the performance of students in the several sections of a course is evaluated and graded with reference to the ability range of the students enrolled and the level of the materials presented in the course. In order to adjust the "bias" against the students in honors courses that results from their competing for grades with peers in the high-ability group, course grades are differentially weighted by the administration in the computation of grade-point averages. Thus, a given grade in an honors course should contribute more to the grade-point average than does the same grade in a regular or opportunity course.

Finally, ability grouping as practiced at Lakeshore High School generally places restrictions upon the grade-point level that a student can attain. Since performance is evaluated and graded relative to the presumed ability range for which the course is designed, a student who is the top performer in an opportunity course would not be accorded the same grade as the best student in an average or honors course. (Theoretically, the former student should be transferred out of the opportunity course to a higher ability section before the end of the semester.) The corollary of this feature of ability grouping should also obtain: The student who performs poorly relative to his peers in an honors course is generally not assigned the lowest absolute grade but one that takes into account the level of the course and the level of the competition. Thus, in practice, there is an implicit "ceiling" and "floor" for grades assigned to students in the various ability sections. The combined effect of the differential *weighting* of grades and the restriction on the *range* of grades assigned is that the high-ability students presumably enjoy an advantage while the low-ability students bear a disadvantage in the competition for grades and academic rank. (Schools that do not prepare a weighted average would tend to create the opposite effect.)

The practice of ability grouping is, of course, directly related to the organizational task of identifying and developing talent in the high school by gearing instruction to the "ability level" of students to prepare them for college entrance. As a preliminary illustration of how ability grouping works, we shall consider the distribution of students in honors courses.

Three honors courses is usually the maximum number that a student is allowed to take at one time at Lakeshore High School. We shall consider students who are enrolled in one or more honors courses as honors students. Although Table 3.4a contains too few

Table 3.4a Distribution of Honors Assignment by Over-all SCAT Scores (Upper Three Classes)*		Table 3.4b Distribution of Honors Assignment by Grade-point Average (Upper Three Classes)†	
SCAT SCORES	NUMBER IN HONORS	GRADE-POINT AVERAGE	NUMBER IN HONORS
91-100	9	1.00-1.50	14
81-90	11	1.75-2.00	12
71-80	10	2.25-3.00	12
66-70	3	3.25	5
N	33	N	43

* One Class IV student with a SCAT score of 68 placed in honors course.
† One Class IV student with grade-point average 1.75 placed in honors course.

cases to do more than illustrate the distribution of honors students by average (over-all) SCAT score categories, it does suggest that SCAT score averages cover a wide range—from 66 to 100.[3]

A similar situation obtains when we contrast junior high school grade-point average and the assignment to honors courses. Table 3.4b shows that the honors students' junior high school grade-point averages cover a wide range—from an *A* (1.00) to less than a *C* (3.25). Two sets of deviant cases are produced by the use of each of the criteria. Table 3.5a presents a list of students who are *not*

---

[3] A SCAT score of 66 or higher is the empirical cut-off point. The official criteria used at Lakeshore High School vary for different courses. The minimum SCAT scores specified for assignment to honors courses may range from 78 to 93.

Table 3.5a Students Not Assigned to Honors Courses with SCAT Scores $\geq$ 66

SCAT	GRADE-POINT AV.	N
90	2.50	1
80	2.25	1
78	1.75	1
75	2.00	1
74	2.00	1
73	2.25	1
68	2.50	3
N		9

Table 3.5b Students Assigned to Honors Courses with Grade-Point Average $\leq$ 2.00

GRADE-POINT AV.	SCAT	N
2.25	(94)(87)(68)	3
2.50	(84)	1
2.60	(96)	1
2.75	(96)(90)(78)(73)(68)(68)	6
3.00	(87)	1
3.25	(93)(90)(78)(75)(75)	5
N		17

in honors courses even though their SCAT scores are 66 or higher. Only two students on this list would also meet the grade-point criterion of 2.00 or higher for honors placement. Table 3.5b presents a list of students who *were* assigned to honors courses even though their grade-point averages were below 2.00, but in each of these cases the SCAT score is 66 or higher.

A tentative statement concerning the assignment of students to honors courses is suggested by our materials: Students who do moderately well on SCAT are generally placed in higher ability classes irrespective of their prior classroom performance, but the student who does poorly on SCAT must have an outstanding grade record to overcome his test performance. There are, however, several cases of honors assignment in which neither SCAT nor grade-point average is high. In our discussion of the assignment of students to ability-grouped sections of courses, we have assumed that SCAT and junior high school grade-point average—the so-called "objective" criteria—are the primary bases for classification and assignment. Our materials illustrate the kinds of discrepancies that can occur and that should be pursued in greater detail. These discrepancies suggest that additional criteria should be explored to account for the distribution of honors and non-honors students.

It is possible that the deviant cases which have appeared in the preceding examination of honors and non-honors assignments are artifacts of our assumption that *over-all* SCAT scores and grade-point *averages* are the criteria used by the school personnel for such assignments. It may be that the component parts of the over-all SCAT scores (i.e., the verbal and quantitative measures) and of the grade-point averages (i.e., grades in English, mathematics, science, etc.) are used as criteria. Our examination of this alternate method of assignment may be found in Table 3.6*a*. The specific

Table 3.6a Distribution of Honors/Non-honors Students by SCAT Scores (Verbal or Quantitative) and Grades in Corresponding Eighth-Grade Subject

| | GRADE A | | | | GRADE B | | | | |
| | SCAT $\geq$ 80 | | SCAT $\leq$ 80 | | SCAT $\geq$ 80 | | SCAT $\leq$ 80 | | |
SUBJECT	H	N-H	H	N-H	H	N-H	H	N-H	N
Algebra	9	1	2	5	13	0	6	17	53
English	7	3	5	1	9	2	0	11	38
Social studies	2	10	2	2	3	6	2	11	38
Science	5	8	0	6	4	4	3	9	38
N	23	22	9	14	29	12	11	48	169

Not recorded in table

> HONORS: One case, SCAT verbal 72, quantitative 89 (no JHS grades available), placed in English, social studies, and mathematics honors
> One case, SCAT quantitative 81, *C* in mathematics
>
> NON-HONORS: One case, SCAT verbal 80, *C* in social studies
> One case, SCAT quantitative 81, *C* in mathematics
> One case, SCAT verbal 87, *D* in English
> One case, SCAT verbal 87, *C* in social studies
> One case, SCAT verbal 87, *C* in English

SCAT scores and course grades of students assigned to the honors sections of each of the four subjects do not differ appreciably from those of non-honors students. The assignment of students with SCAT scores of 80 or above who received an *A* in the related junior high school courses is inconsistent. In algebra, for example, 9 out of 10 students were assigned to honors, while in the other subjects the combination of high SCAT and high grades does not insure assignment to honors. Indeed, in social studies this criterion appears to have little relevance for honors assignment. On the other hand, a SCAT score below 80 and a *B* grade does not disqualify a student from honors except in English. The application of the high specific SCAT score, high course grade criterion produces discrepancies in all four categories in the table. The cell frequencies are, of course, too small to say any more about the discrepancies, but these materials again underline the importance of examining the decision-making activities of the organizational personnel of the high school.

The assignment of students to opportunity sections of courses presents a similar picture. (See Table 3.6*b*.) Students with low

Table 3.6b   Students Assigned to Opportunity Courses by SCAT Scores and Junior High School Grades

	GRADE C				GRADE D				
	SCAT 26–50		SCAT 0–25		SCAT 26–50		SCAT 0–25		
SUBJECT	OPP.	NON-OPP.	OPP.	NON-OPP.	OPP.	NON-OPP.	OPP.	NON-OPP.	N
English*	0	1	1	4	1	0	6	2	15
Social studies	0	0	0	0	0	0	3	0	3
N	0	1	1	4	1	0	9	2	18

* One case assigned to opportunity class in English with verbal SCAT 19 and grade *B* in junior high school English.

SCAT (and STEP) scores and low grades are usually found in such sections, but several discrepancies are again evident. We should note also that there are several further discrepancies that are not shown in this table. Eight students with SCAT and grades comparable to those of students assigned to opportunity sections are enrolled in college or quasi-college preparatory course programs—3 in Type A, 5 in Type B. In addition, 4 other students with comparable SCAT scores and grades were enrolled in Type C, the non-college, non-opportunity-course program. Of these 11 cases, all but one declared an intention to go to college. On the other hand, 5 students who were assigned to opportunity sections also declared their intention to go to college.

Since the assignment of students to opportunity sections reduces their chances of earning high grades and thus improving their academic rank, an opportunity student in such circumstances (quite apart from motivation) would have to perform exceptionally well, if not brilliantly, in order to overcome the limitations imposed upon him by the organization of the ability-grouped curriculums. The obvious point to be made is that if the criteria of ability placement are not clear and consistently applied, the organizational procedures may preclude some students from ever doing better, improving their academic standing, or accumulating college-entrance credits. Conversely, it follows that students whose test scores and grades are comparable to those of students assigned to opportunity sections, but who escape such assignment because of *ad hoc* application of criteria, gain an advantage in the competition for grades and rank within their class. Similar consequences may follow for students assigned to honors courses (as well as those with comparable records who are not assigned to such courses) in a system where higher grades tend routinely to be geared to the level of courses to which they are assigned.

The assignment to honors sections or Type A programs of students whose records show them to have high SCAT scores, high grade-point averages, and college-going intentions presents no problem of interpretation for the organizational personnel. Problems of interpretation and classification arise when the student's records are inconsistent—when, for example, the SCAT score is low and the grade-point average high. The resolution of such "problems" is reflected in the distribution of students among the various organizationally defined categories. It is these distributions that pose problems of explanation for the researcher.

We have attempted thus far, with our limited materials, to illustrate how organizational processes may or may not articulate the college aspirations of students with a program of courses that facilitate the actualization of their educational goals. We have been guided by the question of how similar or comparable "objective" records can result in the classification of students into different categories and assignment to different programs so that their future educational goals are affected.

Given the organization of curriculums at Lakeshore High School, it is obvious that students must be differentiated with reference to their ability by the application of some set of criteria. In this chapter we have examined the "objective" criteria that are presumably applied,[4] but we have not raised the question of the reliability or validity of these criteria as bases for differentiation. Such a discussion would take us too far afield from our primary interests and involve us in controversies that would unnecessarily confuse the issues we wish to examine. Rather, we have examined the organizational limitations imposed by the application of SCAT and grade-point criteria and the opportunities they create for students classified by them. Given these criteria of differentiation, the classification of students activates an organizational recording system that has important feedback effects tending progressively to reinforce the limitations and opportunities of the students' initial placement.

THE EVALUATION OF STUDENT PERFORMANCE

The significance of the differentiation of entering students discussed above may be seen by examination of the periodic evaluation of student performance that is routinely conducted by counseling personnel at Lakeshore High School. We wish, therefore, to investigate how student performances are evaluated by counselors, and how the organizational process of this evaluation further differentiates the student population.

Every student at Lakeshore High is assigned to a counselor who has access to his cumulative school records, containing medical, psychological, social, and personal as well as academic information. One of the duties of the counselor is to review at the end of each marking period the academic progress of the students assigned to

---

[4] It should be noted here that administrators at Lakeshore High School explicitly recognize and encourage the consideration of other criteria, such as the student's "maturity," "intellectual curiosity," range and depth of reading, etc. Because we were unable to study how these and other criteria are implemented by the personnel involved in the initial interpretation procedures, any discussion of their reliability and validity would not be based upon the perspectives of the personnel, but on quite casual information that we obtained indirectly in our study through occasional conversations.

him. Routinely the counselor's review consists primarily of checking the students' grades against their SCAT scores for evidence of "discrepancies." The nature of such discrepancies is noted—e.g., students with high SCAT scores and average or low grades, or average SCAT scores and high grades—and an investigation is initiated by the counselor to determine the bases of the inconsistencies.

From an organizational point of view, the counselor's review of the students' performance constitutes a check upon the effectiveness of the school's program for identifying and developing talent. A large number of SCAT/grade-point discrepancies may be interpreted by the school administrator as evidence that (1) the criterion of "ability" employed is not efficient in differentiating students with different levels of ability, or (2) the "ability" identified by this criterion is not related to the courses that are presumably designed to develop it, or (3) teachers are not performing adequately in developing the ability of students assigned to their courses. Such interpretations of SCAT/grade-point discrepancies would direct the administrator to examine the system for possible methods of improving the "search for talent" program.

On the other hand, SCAT/grade-point discrepancies may be interpreted as *characteristics of students.* That is, the efficiency of the tests used to identify ability, the courses designed to develop it, and the teachers assigned to evaluate the degree of development is not questioned. Rather, what is questioned is the students' failure to perform "up to their ability." An interesting feature of our study is that references to inadequacies, defects, or failures of the "system" by organizational personnel were virtually absent. When such references were made, they were *ad hoc* or *ad hominem* comments concerning, for example, some student who was "mistakenly" assigned by "someone" to a higher or lower section than he should have been, or some student who is "really much better than those test results indicate," or some teacher who expects more or less of his students than he should. In short, the characteristic interpretation made by counselors and other school personnel of SCAT/grade-point discrepancies is that students perform below or above their tested ability as a consequence of motivational, personal, and social "problems," not methods of teaching, preparation (readiness), or aptitude.

In order to obtain information concerning the process of student evaluation as practiced by the counseling personnel, we systematically questioned the counselor to whom the students in our sample were assigned. We were particularly interested in the criteria used in categorizing student achievement and in how the achievement-type classification compares with the "objective" measures of student ability (SCAT) and performance (grade-point average in the freshman year). The materials obtained in our interviews with this counselor are presented below.

The counselor's achievement types. When we asked the counselor how she would classify each of the students in our sample,[5] she employed the following categories (which were widely used by the teaching as well as the counseling personnel at Lakeshore High) of classification: (1) "Excellent student," (2) "Average achiever," (3) "Underachiever," (4) "Overachiever," (5) "Opportunity student." Asked what she considered the most stable basis for her judgment of a student, she replied:

"Probably ability—that's the most specific and measurable."
Interviewer: "And how do you determine ability?"
Counselor: "By tests and performance, generally."

If we assume that the counselor's evaluation of student performance is to assess the students' progress in the courses to which they have been assigned, we would expect a systematic relationship between the achievement-type classification and the distribution of SCAT/grade-point discrepancies. In Table 3.7 we have included the SCAT scores and grade-point averages of each of the students classified by the counselor in order to show the relation between discrepancies and achievement types. An examination of the table will show the range of discrepancies classified in the five achievement types by the counselor. (The range of discrepancies for each

5 The counselor did not classify 7 students for various reasons, such as drop-outs, transfers to another division, and no information.

Table 3.7   Counselor's Achievement Types by SCAT Scores and Ninth-grade Point Average

ACHIEVEMENT TYPES	NINTH-GRADE POINT AVERAGE					N
	1.00–1.50	1.75–2.00	2.25–3.00	3.25–4.00	4.25–5.00	
Opportunity student			(15)	(06)(10) (12)(16)	(01)(02) (02)(13)	9
Overachiever		(42)	(27)	(16)		3
Underachiever		(68)	(68)(68) (73)(80)(84) (87)(90)(96)	(17)(39) (58)(75)(78) (80)(93)	(10)(39)	18
Average achiever		(47)(64) (64)(75)	(27)(32)(35) (39)(50)(64) (64)(68)(68) (68)(68)(73) (73)(78)(84) (87)(90)	(15)(20)(20) (35)(42)(42) (50)(52)(54) (75)	(28) (39)	33
Excellent student	(73)(73)(80) (84)(85)(94) (95)(97)	(75)(78) (84)(84) (90)(93) (95)(96)	(94)	(90)		18
N	8	14	28	23	9	81*

* No information for 8 cases.

category of achievement types is summarized in Table 3.8.)   For example, the "excellent student" category includes 9 students with SCAT scores of 90–95 and with grade-point averages ranging from 1.00 to 3.25.   On the other hand, the 2.25–3.00 grade point column

Table 3.8   Range of SCAT and Ninth-grade Point Average by Counselor's Classification of Achievement Types

ACHIEVEMENT TYPES	SCAT RANGE	GRADE-POINT RANGE	N
Excellent student	73–97	1.00–3.25	18
Average achiever	15–90	1.75–4.25	33
Underachiever	10–96	2.00–4.66	18
Overachiever	16–42	2.00–3.75	3
Opportunity student	01–16	3.00–5.00	9
			81*

* No information for 8 cases.

shows that there are 4 students with SCAT scores of 90–95, but 2 are classified as "underachievers," another as an "average achiever," and the fourth as an "excellent student." These classifications are not a strict application of the SCAT/grade-point discrepancy criterion. The classification of other students (e.g., the SCAT 68/1.75–2.00 "underachiever," the SCAT 17/3.25–4.00 "underachiever," the SCAT 47/1.75–2.00 "average achiever," etc.) provides added evidence that the criterion is not consistently applied and does not account for the distribution of achievement types. The table shows that neither SCAT nor grade point alone accounts for the achievement-type classifications.

The inconsistencies revealed in this classification of students are of more than passing interest, for the achievement types are not merely descriptive categories to the personnel who use them. The classification of students as achievement types in effect produces a distribution of students who are conceived by the organizational personnel to have "problems." With the exception of students classified, by whatever criteria, as "average achiever" and "excellent student," the achievement-type classification identifies those students who are performing below the level of their ability ("underachiever") or above it ("overachiever"), or who are lacking in both ability and performance ("opportunity student"). In the following chapter we shall discuss how these "problems" are articulated with the organizational activities of counselors at Lakeshore High and 19 other high schools. We wish here to pursue further the criteria applied in the process of evaluating student performance.

If the more or less "rational criterion" of SCAT/grade-point discrepancy does not account for the counselor's achievement-type classification of students, what are the bases of her judgments? What are the variables that might operate to produce the variations in the distribution discussed above? Social-class characteristics of the student population, commonly found by social researchers to influence the evaluations of students by school personnel, are variables that deserve examination. In our investigation of this possibility we were directed by our theoretical orientation, which emphasizes the vocabulary and syntax used by the organizational personnel, to obtain the social-class categories that *the counselor* used to differentiate the student population.

The counselor's social types. To explore the relation between the stratification system as perceived by the counselor and her classification of achievement types, we questioned her as follows:

a: How many social statuses, that is, social-class groups, would you say there are here at Lakeshore High School?

b: How would you describe, in general, each of the groups you mentioned?

c: How would you place each of the students named on these cards (handing her a set of cards with the names of all the students in our sample) into each of the groups you mentioned?

The phrasing of the questions assumes that social-status categories are recognized, if not employed, by the counselor as one dimension of her classification of students. The questions, however, allow the counselor to interpret "social status, that is, social-class groups" in her own terms. We would expect the counselor to base her evaluations on the same kind of common-sense criteria one would expect from persons in the general population—i.e., the categories and criteria should be characteristically general, vaguely defined, and perhaps inconsistently applied.

When the counselor was asked question *a*, she offered without prompting from the interviewer a description of each group as she identified them. That is, the interviewer found it unnecessary to ask question *b*. The counselor's categories and comments were as follows:

1. First there's the main group—the in-group. This is the group that belongs to the "Y." They head this group, they're at the forefront of the activities in the school, they're the leaders. Most of them live in Lakeshore. They belong to the Presbyterian Church there, or is it a Methodist Church?

2. Then there's the group just below this group. They're trying to attain the [main] group. They're sometimes included in the activities of the first group, but they don't really belong. They might be the campaign managers for members of the first group if they're running for an office. This group will do almost anything to get into the other group.

3. There's the other element. These students would not at all consider

getting into the first group. They get into a lot of trouble, they have difficulties with their studies. Most of the drop-outs are from this group—they drop out at 16 or 17.

4. We can't deny that there's a Negro group here at Lakeshore. They have their own group, their own identification. In some instances there are those who cut across the line, but they don't participate in their "Y" activities. The "Y" seems to be the center of activities, and the "Y" is a segregated group.

5. Then there's the group that's left [not politically left, but left by subtraction]. This is not really a group. They don't have a group of their own. There are some strong individualists in this group.

6. We should make some note of those other students who are not in a group. They are noteworthy individuals. Because they are outstanding they are known to everybody. But they don't belong to any group. They're the kind that might wear black leotards or carry a guitar. They're a group, but not a group. They come to our attention in some way—they're outstanding scholastically, or they're extremely sensitive, [the counselor smiled here, which was interpreted to mean that she did not want to be more explicit] or intelligent. Some of them are referred for psychiatric care. [The counselor cited the case of a student in our sample who would fit this group. She called this group "loners."]

7. [The counselor then mentioned another group who were "like loners" but she said they were "rebelling." This group dressed, she said, in extreme fashion.] They wear their skirts too short. [In our sample, this group consists of four or five girls who are described as being tightly banded together, but who are not thought to have the "nerve" to do anything as individuals.] They find it difficult to fit into things at Lakeshore High. Anything typical of teen-agers here is ridiculous for them. [The counselor stated that the "loner" described in the last group might wear leotards or braids or carry a guitar even if no one else were doing so.]

The counselor's response to question *a* indicates that she interpreted "social status, that is, social class" to mean different *social types* of students within the stratification system of the high school, and we shall refer to them hereafter by that term. With the exception of Social Types *1* and *2*, and perhaps the "Negro group" (Social Type *4*), her descriptions do not necessarily imply a strict hierarchical ranking in the conventional terms of social class. The pluralistic classification appears to be based on some combination of aspiration, rejection, or withdrawal of students from participation in school and out-of-school social activities.

In response to question *c,* the counselor classified the students in our sample into the categories that she enumerated and described. Table 3.9 shows the relation between her social-type and

Table 3.9   Counselor's Social Types by Counselor's Classification of Achievement Designations

SOCIAL TYPES	ACHIEVEMENT TYPES					
	EXCEL.	AVER.	UNDER	OVER	OPPOR.	N
7	0	1	0	1	1	3
6	1	0	0	0	0	1
5	0	10	7	1	4	22
4	0	1	0	0	2	3
3	0	2	4	0	1	7
2	4	16	6	1	2	29
1	12	2	1	0	0	15
N	17	32	18	3	10	80*

* No information on 9 cases.

achievement-type classifications of students. Twelve of the 17 students classified as "excellent students" were also classified as Social Type *1.* Conversely, all but 3 of the 15 Social Type *1* students were classified as "excellent students." In none of the remaining categories in which the frequencies are large enough to warrant consideration (i.e., Social Types *2* and *5,* and the achievement types of "average achiever" and "underachiever") is there a suggested relationship which approaches that between the "excellent student"—Social Type *1* classification.

It would appear that there is a fusion of academic and social-type criteria in the counselor's classification of the "excellent" Social Type *1* student. Table 3.10, which presents the distribution of social types with reference to the students' SCAT scores and grade-point averages, provides a clue to the nature of the academic criteria that may have been applied by the counselor in the social-type classification. With one exception (one student with SCAT of 68), all students in Social Type *1* have SCAT scores of 73 or higher, but their grade-point averages range from 1.00 to 4.00. The classification of the 94/2.25–3.00 student and the 90/3.25–4.00 student in Social Type *1* shows that these relatively large SCAT/grade-point

Table 3.10 Counselor's Social Types by SCAT Scores and Ninth-grade Point Average

SOCIAL TYPE	NINTH-GRADE POINT AVERAGE					N
	1.00–1.50	1.75–2.00	2.25–3.00	3.25–4.00	4.25–5.00	
7				(15)	(13)	2
6	(97)					1
5		(47)	(15)(27) (32)(39)(64) (68)(68)(73) (80)	(17)(20) (35)(52) (58)	(02)(07) (10)	18
4			(78)	(06)(50)	(01)	4
3				(10)(12) (39)(42) (54)(78)	(39)	7
2	(85)	(42)(64) (64)(75) (90)(93)	(27)(35)(50) (64)(68)(68) (84)(84)(87) (87)(90)(90) (96)	(16)(20) (42)(75) (93)	(02)	26
1	(73)(73) (80)(84) (94)(95)	(68)(75) (78)(84) (84)(95) (96)	(73)(73) (94)	(75)(90)		18
N	8	14	27	21	7	76*

* No information for 13 cases.

discrepancies (indicating underachievement) did not disqualify them from inclusion in this category. We note, however, that although high SCAT appears to be a characteristic of Social Type *1* students, there is an equal number of students with scores of 73 or higher who were classified in other social-type categories.

The characterization of the "excellent" Social Type *1* student that may be made from Tables 3.9 and 3.10 is that of a student whom the counselor considers to be a "leader," who is in the "main group," and who has a relatively high SCAT score even if he does not have a high grade-point average. Table 3.10 also indicates that neither SCAT nor grade-point average separately nor the discrepancy between them is systematically related to the classification of social types. Our materials suggest that the counselor's social-type classification does not account for the majority of her achievement-type classification of students.

The counselor's social-class ratings. The counselor's response to question *a* raised the question of whether or not she differentiated students by social-class categories in the conventional sense. If so, would her classification of students in those terms better account for the achievement types than the social types? To obtain this information, we explained to the counselor that we would like her to classify our student sample into five strata of social classes. Using a fivefold classification, we presented these strata to her as: Class I, Upper; Class II, Lower Upper; Class III, Upper Middle; Class IV, Lower Middle; and Class V, Lower. No further criteria for the classification of students, except as indicated immediately below, were given to the counselor. When she was presented with these strata, the counselor asked:

> What do you mean by "upper"? In Lakeshore that would have to be old-guard Lakeshore. There may be some with more money, but they wouldn't be old guard. For example, the ——— boy's family has lots of money, but they don't make it on the old guard.
> *Interviewer:* So, the ——— boy would not be placed in the "upper" class if that's true.

Table 3.11 shows the social-class distribution that resulted from the counselor's classification of students by achievement-type categories. It should be noted that although the counselor indicated by her remark about the "old-guard Lakeshore" that she recognized

Table 3.11   Distribution of Achievement Types by Counselor's Social-class Ratings

ACHIEVEMENT TYPES	COUNSELOR'S SOCIAL-CLASS RATINGS					
	I	II	III	IV	V	N
Opportunity		2	1	4	2	9
Overachiever		2	1			3
Underachiever		10	5	4		19
Average achiever		12	13	5	1	31
Excellent		17	1			18
N		42	21	13	3	80*

* No information on 9 cases.

the existence of an "upper" class, she did not assign any of the students in our sample to that social class. As in the case of Social Type *1*, "excellent students" are predominantly from one category—all but one in Social Class II. The converse relationship, however, does not obtain: i.e., only 40 per cent (17 out of 42) Class II students are classified as "excellent students." Thus, although the social-class category adds the characteristic of Social Class II to the description of the "excellent student," it does no better than the social-type classification in suggesting the basis for the over-all distribution of achievement types.

THE BASES OF THE COUNSELOR'S JUDGMENTS

In our discussion of the routine organizational evaluation of student performance at Lakeshore High School, we have focused our attention on the distribution of achievement types that is produced by the evaluation process. We have attempted to account for this distribution by a consideration of (1) the more or less "objective" criterion of SCAT/grade-point discrepancy which, given the method of assigning students to courses at this school, is presumably applied in the evaluation process; (2) the counselor's social-type classification of students, on the assumption that more "subjective" factors enter into her evaluation of students; and (3) the counselor's social-class classification, to assess the importance of this often discussed variable. Our materials suggest that the counselor's achievement-type classification of students is a product of a subtle fusion of "rational" and common-sense judgments. Belonging to the "in-group" may be given greater weight than grade-point average in classifying a student as an "excellent student," or "getting into a lot of trouble" may be more important than "performing up to ability level" in deciding that a student is an "underachiever."

The tables that we have presented and discussed clearly do not reveal the subtleties that contribute to the counselor's assessment and interpretations of student performance. In the following chapter, we shall explore these subtleties in some detail by examining interview materials obtained from two samples of counselors. We shall present here, however, a few of the counselor's comments concerning students in our sample in order to illustrate the variety of criteria that are implicitly or explicitly applied by the counselor in the evaluation process. These illustrative cases were selected from the counselor's response to our request that she tell us what she knew about each of the students in our sample.

CASE 10: SCAT 90/Grade Point 2.75, Social Class II, Social Type *2*. *"Underachiever."* His mother says he is a pleasant, outgoing boy. His teachers will say he's either a pleasant boy or that he's a pest. I think he's arrogant. He thinks he's handsome. He's nice-looking, but not handsome. He thinks he owns Lakeshore. He talks to his teachers as if they were stupid. He's a good student. He's in biology and algebra honors.
Interviewer: Is he going to college?
He plans college. I think he said he plans to go East like MIT, Harvard, etc. He won't make it. He's a candidate for a middle-western school. I think they'll all go to college. It's a matter of which one and for how long.

CASE 13: SCAT 90/Grade Point 3.25, Social Class II, Social Type *1*. *"Excellent student."* She's a very intelligent little girl. She's in all honors. They're an academic family. She's a mousy little girl. Maybe in time she'll develop socially. Her parents were concerned about her grade in English. They felt she could get a 1 instead of a 2. She got a 1 this time. And, of course, she'll go to college.

CASE 30: SCAT 93/Grade Point 2.00, Social Class II, Social Type *2*. *"Excellent student."* ―――― is a very able student. Kind of like an old man. Like he doesn't know how to have fun. He's always worried about doing the right thing. He came in and worried about which club to join because of how it would look for his college record, not for fun. I think he works after school in a store. It's as if he had to keep quiet all his life.

CASE 33: SCAT 75/Grade Point 2.00. Social Class III, Social Type *2*. *"Average achiever."* A very quiet girl. She doesn't come in very often. She'll go to college. She's in the highest honors in algebra but that's all. She's so quiet she probably goes unnoticed.

CASE 35: SCAT 20/Grade Point 4.00, Social Class II, Social Type *2*. *"Average achiever."* I just talked to her mother. A nice little girl. Not too bright. Her parents want her to go to college. She doesn't do too well. She's very enthusiastic about school. She'll probably go to ――――, an expensive junior college in the East. It requires 4 years of English and graduation from high school. Her sister went there. Her mother is very realistic about this. ―――― is like a finishing school.
Interviewer: Where is this college?

[The counselor looks it up.] Oh, it's in ———. I thought it was in the East. She comes in very often with small things that I can answer very quickly. She has troubles—she fails classes. She failed algebra, tutor and all, and had to switch to general math.

CASE 70: SCAT 10/Grade Point 4.66, Social Class II, Social Type 5. *"Underachiever."* She's an opportunity student. She's a very conscientious girl. She tries hard, does neat work. She plans to go to college— she may get into some small junior college. She's very concerned at this point.
Interviewer: How do her parents feel?
I don't know—I haven't contacted them about it. I feel if her parents are concerned they will contact the school. Apparently they're not concerned. Or her parents might be concerned—some parents don't come in. She works hard—she'll probably benefit from some nonacademic college. [Looking at the record] Her father's senior vice president of ——— ——— [a large corporation]—my, I didn't realize. He's been to college and her mother went to high school.

The discussion in this chapter may be summarized as follows:
1. Our examination of the ascription hypothesis in Chapter 2 indicated that the relation between student and parental college-going aspirations and their implementation of those aspirations must be viewed as problematic. In the present chapter, we have stressed the point that, given the formal declaration of such aspirations, the implementation of the declaration is contingent upon the organizational procedures that launch freshmen students toward their educational goals. These contingencies are created by the educational doctrines of the school, the organization of its curriculums, and the routines of bureaucratic procedures in which "objective" and "subjective" criteria are combined in the processing of students through the system. The question we have explored is not how the school does or does not manage to process students independently of the students' declared educational aspirations. Rather, we have been concerned with how the school as a bureaucratic organization incorporates in its rules and procedures the processes by which the aspirations of students are recorded, their ability assessed, and their performance evaluated.
2. We have presented materials to illustrate the diffuse character of the criteria used in assigning students to types of programs and

courses, and we have discussed the implications of this assignment procedure for the progress of students toward their declared educational goals. Our materials indicate also that the criteria used to evaluate the subsequent performance of students are equally diffuse and that the evaluation process makes the realization of those goals problematic. We have illustrated how the rationale of ability grouping organizationally produces and defines instances of SCAT/ grade-point discrepancies as "problems" to be identified and classified by the counselor. In addition to the "objective" data of the SCAT/grade-point discrepancy, the counselor must somehow decide the relevance of a variety of noncomparable factors for her evaluation of the students' performance. Such factors as the comments of teachers concerning students, the expressed concern of parents regarding the prospects of realizing their plans for sending their children to college, information about a student's "delinquent" activities, and the like may implicitly or explicitly enter into her evaluations. The limitations of resources and time do not allow the counselor to "objectively" weigh and give weightings to the variety of information considered relevant for the evaluation. The task of "objectifying" the bases of such decisions is clearly a difficult if not an impossible one.[6]

3. We have suggested that the differentiation of students produced by the evaluation process is directly related to the organizational effort to identify and develop talent, because the categories of differentiation are defined in terms of a presumed relationship between ability and performance. The classification of students differentiates those who are and are not "having trouble." The evaluation of student performance and the classification it pro-

---

[6] This problem is not unique to the counselor but in various forms confronts other personnel at Lakeshore High School. For example, the official criteria presented to personnel to guide their placement of students in English honors sections states: "1. Have received a grade of *A* for their English work in the eighth grade. 2. Write well. 3. Appreciate good literature. 4. Read widely and well. 5. Are not 'grade-grubbers.' 6. Reason with logic in advance of their years. 7. Participate thoughtfully in class discussion. 8. Are emotionally and intellectually mature for their age. 9. Are intellectually curious. 10. Are well motivated and enjoy English." (Quoted from Lakeshore High placement criteria as developed by the English Department for selection of incoming freshmen for English honors advanced placement.)

duces has more than nominal significance for the future educational, occupational, and life careers of students. In a bureaucratically organized school such as Lakeshore High, the classification of students routinely initiates organizational actions that may progressively define and limit the development of such careers. From this perspective, the criteria employed in the evaluation process, the information considered relevant and recorded, the interpretations made of such information, and the organizationally defined categories by which students are classified are important for an understanding of how the school produces senior students who are or are not qualified for college entrance, "highly recommended" or "poor prospects," "well-rounded personalities" or "maladjusted."

4. THE BUREAUCRATIZATION

OF THE COUNSELING SYSTEM

In our exploration of the organizational processes of evaluating and classifying students, we have focused on the activities of the counselors at Lakeshore High School. In view of the strategic importance of such activities for the movement of students through the school system, we wish now to examine in greater detail the development of student counseling as a specialized activity in school organization, the status of counselors within that organization, and the professional orientations that guide the descriptions, interpretations, and treatment of the problems they handle. More specifically, we shall discuss the activities of counselors as they affect the college-going aspirations of students and their parents, the identification of academic and other problems, the sponsorship of students through high school and into college, and by implication, the channeling of students toward various educational, occupational, and life careers.

COUNSELING IN THE SCHOOL SYSTEM

High school counseling is in a period of transition from semi-professional status, characterized by a range of activities performed by variously trained persons in conjunction with other duties, to an increasingly professional status of considerable authority and prestige within the educational system of the United States. This increased professionalization of the counseling system is in part a consequence of the bureaucratization of the educational system in general, and it is of interest to the sociologist in two ways. First, the professionalization of counseling activities is of interest to sociologists who study the emergence, development, and change of occupations. Second, for students of social stratification, the growth of counseling in the educational system poses the question of whether and how counseling activities affect the student's status in the high school and in turn his later educational, occupational, and life careers.

Counseling and the search for talent.   High school counseling in the United States has received considerable support from what has been described as the "crisis in education." The popular conception of a race with foreign powers for the production of technical competence presumably provides an important rationale for public discourse concerning the "crisis." Educators, officials at all levels of government, and assorted commentators express the concern that the nation's talent is not being developed and utilized to its fullest extent. If talent exists that is not being utilized it logically follows that personnel must be recruited and trained to expedite the identification and channeling of that talent into careers to insure its most productive use. Thus, one important consequence of the concern for the identification and development of talent has been an increase in interest and support for the expansion of counseling services within the school system. The National Defense Education Act of 1958 explicitly provides funds for such expansion.

Even before the current "crisis," however, the teacher-counselor in the school system performed many of the duties that are now assumed by counselors. In the pre-war organization of school systems, the activities now formally recognized and designated as the domain of the counselor were performed by classroom teachers and administrators. The teacher often nursed minor injuries, advised students on personal and academic problems, imposed minor disciplinary measures, and acted as parental surrogate in addition to performing her instructional duties. The increased size and bureaucratization of the school led to the development of "home-rooms" which were designed to carry out administrative policies and to coordinate general student and school activities. The home-room teacher began to be assigned more specialized duties and also to assume greater responsibility for handling academic and personal problems. In this process, the homeroom teacher became the teacher-counselor. Even in schools in which tests were administered by specialized testing psychologists, the activities of the homeroom teacher and teacher-counselor gradually subsumed interpreting the results of intelligence, aptitude, achievement, and other tests to students and parents and advising them on curriculum and voca-tional careers.

Further increases in the scale of organization led to reduction in teaching duties to enable teacher-counselors to handle the increas-ingly time-consuming tasks associated with testing, academic and vocational guidance, record-keeping, and other clerical work. Al-though the more traditional teacher-counselor is retained in many high school systems throughout the country, the large urban, com-prehensive high schools are moving in the direction of more coun-selor-teachers whose time is specifically allocated between teaching and counseling duties. This movement in the direction of more and more full-time counselors in the high school (and even the junior high school), has been accomplished by increased specializa-tion. It should be noted, however, that this trend was well under way prior to the so-called "crisis."

THE PROFESSIONALIZATION OF COUNSELING

Since before World War II guidance counselors have been active in seeking professional status through certification and licensing, and the growing demand for their services by school systems has rein-forced and intensified these efforts toward professionalization. The literature on counseling and guidance in the school system contains extensive discussions of problems of standardizing professional training and certification procedures, defining the professional domain of the counselor's competence and authority, and legitimizing the counselor's activities within that domain.[1] The efforts of counselors to achieve professional status have involved them in a conflict of interest with other professionals such as psychiatrists, clinical psychologists, and social workers, all of whom engage in activity defined as therapy.

The conflict of interests is intensified by differences in state requirements for guidance counselors in school systems. Some states issue certificates for professional counselors, but not always for the same kind of activity. The lack of certification standards, or the lack of enforcement where such standards exist, prevents professional counseling groups or groups that aspire to professional status from controlling the recruitment and activities of high school counselors. For example, a high school administrator may assign counseling duties to selected teachers without regard to their professional training or competence as counselors. When the various professional counseling organizations themselves differ with regard to standards of certification, the high school administrator may define and apply his own set of qualification criteria to recruit counseling personnel. An administrator may decide against hiring a certified counselor as an expensive educational "frill," choose a counselor of one professional persuasion over another as an expe-

---

[1] For discussions of problems of professionalization in general see Talcott Parsons, *Essays in Sociological Theory*. Glencoe: Free Press, 1954, ch. II; Theodore Caplow, *The Sociology of Work*. Minneapolis: University of Minnesota Press, 1954, pp. 139-140; Morris L. Cogan, "The Problem of Defining a Profession," *Annals of the Amer. Acad. of Political and Social Science*, Jan. 1955, pp. 105-111; Ernest Greenwood, "Attributes of a Profession," *Social Work*, July 1957, pp. 45-55; Roy Lewis and Angus Maude, *Professional People in England*. Cambridge: Harvard University Press, 1953; Donald R. Cressey, "Professional Correctional Work and Professional Work in Correction," *National Probation and Parole Assoc. Jour.*, 5, Jan. 1959, pp. 1-15; William J. Goode, "Community Within a Community: The Professions," *Amer. Sociological Rev.*, 22, April 1957, pp. 194-200; Mary Jean Huntington, "Sociology of Professions, 1945-55," in Hans L. Zetterberg, *Sociology in the United States of America*. Paris: UNESCO, 1956, pp. 87-93. A survey of the literature on the professionalization of counseling and guidance in the school system is presented in *The Review of Educational Research*, 30, April 1960. See also David M. Trout, "Why Define Counseling in Medical Terms?," *The Personnel and Guidance Jour.*, 32, May 1954, pp. 518-523; Ellis D. Tooker, "Counselor Role: Counselor Training," *Personnel and Guidance Jour.*, 36 Dec. 1957, pp. 263-267.

dient method of dealing with scarcity of available personnel, or appoint teachers to counseling positions as a means of exercising greater control over the counseling staff.

The ambiguous professional status of counselors is also reflected in the range of duties they are assigned within the school system. Although most school administrators have accepted the notion that some kind of counseling is necessary, the kind may vary from state to state and from one school district to the next. For example, a school may have only part-time teacher-counselors who have taken summer courses in such subjects as psychological testing, vocational counseling, or guidance. Teacher-counselors with such training may handle a wide range of student problems, from delinquency to college or vocational guidance. In more highly bureaucratized schools, three groups of counselors may be differentiated organizationally: One group may deal with formal testing and related consultative work; another group may handle "deep emotional" problems; and a third group may be concerned with programming students into college and vocational courses and with related counseling activities. This three-way division of counseling activities, as we shall see, is closely connected with the professionalization of counseling.

It is, however, the counseling of students with a wide range of so-called "emotional" problems on which the conflict of professional interests is primarily focused. The claims of social workers and psychologists to therapy functions are well known, and within the school system they are presumably more competent than the counselors to handle the "deep emotional" problems. In their attempts to define a professional domain, therefore, school counselors have been concerned with establishing a claim to what we may term "surface" problems that students may encounter in their day-to-day school and extracurricular activities. It should be noted, however, that in a highly bureaucratized school system the counselor occupies a position in which he coordinates the referral of students to the various special services, including those of the psychologists and social workers. The position of coordinator enables the counselor, intentionally or otherwise, to define as "surface" a range of student problems that the social worker, psychologist, or psychiatrist might diagnose as "deep" problems requiring professional therapy.

In this situation of interprofessional rivalry, the counselor seeks to develop his own definitions of problem types that will not conflict with or overlap those used by social workers, psychologists, and psychiatrists. Such definitions would presumably fall somewhere between *social types* and *clinical types*. We are assuming that teachers and counselors of an earlier period conceived, characterized, and interpreted student problems in everyday terminology and related them to the everyday activities of the classroom, the peer group, and the home. For example, students might be called "lazy," "indifferent," "wild," "girl crazy," "unhappy at home," and the like. A clinical approach to these same problems would presumably describe them in terms that imply more serious roots and consequences. In the terminology of clinical types, a child may be "rejected," "overly dependent," "weak in ego strength," have an "unresolved Oedipus problem," and the like.

One of the basic theoretical interests guiding the formulation of our research design was the question of the extent to which "clinical" and "social" types become fused in the description, interpretation, and treatment of student problems by counselors, social workers, and psychologists. We assumed that the "crisis" in education has increased efforts to identify talent by the use of existing techniques and methods, primarily the various psychological and achievement tests. We also assumed that counselors have been assigned the organizational task of monitoring the academic progress of students, identifying and advising them on their difficulties, and recommending remedial actions to administrative and teaching personnel. We sought to obtain data on this activity by focusing upon the organizational status of counselors in the high school and the ways in which problems are handled by the several types of special-services personnel.

It is our thesis that the bureaucratization of the counseling system in large, comprehensive high schools leads to an emphasis upon and concern for professional status among counselors, and that this professionalization will produce a greater range and frequency of student problems (e.g., over- and underachievers) than in schools in which counseling duties are assigned to and performed by less professionalized teacher-counselors. Furthermore, there should be a specific emphasis upon defining the academic difficulties of students in clinical terms, and this emphasis should significantly affect the processing of students in the search for talent, the differential sponsorship of students to higher educational opportunities, and the processes of social mobility within the larger society.

THE ORGANIZATIONAL STATUS OF THE COUNSELOR

The staff functions of the counselor may vary from extensive teaching with time off for counseling duties to no teaching and many additional administrative duties. The less teaching that counselors do, the more antagonism they are likely to encounter vis-à-vis teachers whose cooperation and assistance are essential for the performance of their counseling activities. Often the teacher feels that the counselor cannot understand the student unless the student's actual classroom conduct is observed, including student-teacher interactions. The fact that many counselors are ex-teachers while others are "fresh out of graduate school" with graduate degrees in counseling leads to further ambiguity in their organizational status. They often invoke both their teacher and counselor credentials to legitimize their counseling activities. Social workers and psychologists have more professionalized status in the eyes of teachers, but they are still considered inexperienced in their knowledge of classroom activities.

Because counselors may be assigned part-time administrative duties and later be promoted to full-time administrative positions, they are often able to marshal strategic political support for their activities. The counselors' organizational position brings them into closer working association with the administrative personnel than with the teaching staff, and the administrator comes to rely upon counselors for information that he formerly obtained from teachers. In such circumstances, evaluations of students, assignment to courses, transfers, and other academic matters are increasingly decided by the counselor and administrator in consultation. Although this division of functions allows teachers to concentrate their efforts on their specific instructional duties, they may nevertheless view it with displeasure as well as relief, for it diminishes their influence and authority vis-à-vis the student. The reduction of such influence and authority in turn tends to downgrade the teacher's organizational position in the school system. The teacher may be requested, if not required, to communicate his observations and assessments of students to counselors and to consult the latter about decisions that the teacher may feel more qualified to make. To the teacher who already feels that the administration intrudes too often upon his domain, the counselor may be *persona non grata*.

Counseling activities and organizational routines.   In order to understand the organizational status of the counselor, it is necessary to examine some of the problems that arise in daily routines. The counselor must face the problem of creating an atmosphere of "professional confidence." One aspect of professional confidence is the control of various kinds of information obtained about the student. In the course of an interview with the counselor, the student may reveal information about teachers, other counselors, or administrators. Such information can lead the counselor to investigate and form judgments about the competence of teachers and other school personnel in their handling of the student in question. Thus, by virtue of their professional activities, counselors occupy a position in the communication network of the school system that adds to the ambiguity of their relations with other school personnel.

Since counselors are often originally appointed to positions on the teaching staff, their subsequent assignment to counseling duties is compensated for by reductions of their teaching responsibilities. The time free from teaching and other duties that counselors are allowed generally increases with the case loads they are assigned. The allocation of such free time, which teachers may view as disproportionate to the work counselors do, serves to remind other school personnel of the administration's recognition of the professional nature of counseling. The time off granted to counselors may thus become a focus of resentment on the part of teachers who are already sensitive to the counselor's organizational influence, and may further differentiate counselors in the status hierarchy of the school.

Our investigation of the activities and status of counselors in the school system was guided by several questions that we hoped would pinpoint the problems discussed above and relate them to our larger concern with the bureaucratization of the high school and the differentiation of the student population:

1. What skills and technical knowledge are necessary to become a high school counselor, and how do counselors acquire them? How is the acquisition of such skills and technical knowledge related to the conflicting professional interests of counselors, social workers, psychologists, and psychiatrists?
2. What different procedures do counselors follow in the receiving, handling, and disposing of students? How do the kinds of students seen, and the specialized techniques utilized, provide the substantive and organizational basis for the development of an autonomous profession? How does the professionalization of counseling activities create organizational contingencies for the implementation of student aspirations to go to college?
3. How can administrative decisions as to which personnel will handle various student problems influence the status of the counselor in the organizational hierarchy of the school? How does the allocation of such duties affect the range and frequency of the types of student problems which are organizationally defined and treated?

The remainder of this chapter will be devoted to a presentation of illustrative materials from our interviews with two small samples of high school counselors. One sample is a group of 19 counselors[2] who attended a training program for high school guidance personnel at Northwestern University during the period of our study. The second sample of 21 includes all the counselors employed at Lakeshore High School, with one exception. (The exception, a part-time counselor, declined to be interviewed.) We also inter-

2 The high schools represented by these counselors enrolled from 250 to 3000 students. The schools were located in 19 states, including Arkansas, Indiana (2), Kansas, Michigan (3), Missouri (2), Nebraska, New Mexico, North Dakota (2), Ohio (2), Oklahoma, West Virginia, and Wisconsin (2). This group of counselors was interviewed by Rose Giallombardo, whose assistance we gratefully acknowledge.

viewed the four social workers who counsel students at Lakeshore High.

The professional perspectives of counselors.   Three types of counselors may be distinguished from the interviews with the Lakeshore High counselors, as well as with the 19 in what we shall hereafter call the "outside" sample. The first type includes teachers whose primary duties are concerned with classroom teaching but who counsel for about an hour each day. We shall call this group "teacher-counselors." The second group we call "counselor-teachers" because their primary duty is to counsel students, although they also teach one or two courses each day. The third group, which we call "counselors," are personnel who devote full time to counseling activities.

We have arbitrarily selected four interview protocols for use as illustrations of the responses of the three types of counseling personnel to our questions, and a fifth to present the perspectives of social workers. We shall refer to them as Cases 1 through 5. From the outside sample, we have selected two to illustrate the more traditionally oriented teacher-counselor conceptions of students, and from our Lakeshore High three interviews for illustrating the more clinical orientation of full-time counselors and social workers. The two cases from the outside sample are a teacher-counselor (Case 1) employed in a school with a student population of 600, and a counselor-teacher (Case 2) from a school enrolling 1500 students. From Lakeshore we have selected a counselor-teacher (Case 3) and a counselor (Case 4). Case 5 is a social worker at Lakeshore High.

The following questions were asked to obtain information on the professional perspectives of counselors:

> *a:* How did you get into counseling?
> *b:* Are there any special requirements for counselors at this (your) school?
> *c:* What kind of training do you think a counselor should have?[3]

CASE 1:

> *a:* Well, that's a good question—I think my first year in teaching. I had an interest in this sort of thing and after I had worked as an advisor

[3]This question was not asked of counselors in the "outside" sample. None of the three questions above was asked of social workers.

for a year, I realized I wouldn't want to be a classroom teacher the rest of my life.

b: An M.A. and a state certificate in counseling.

CASE 2:

a: I got into it through teaching. I was teaching social studies and had gotten into the vocational school. The principal thought we should give more time to orientation. The principal thought I could handle it, so I joined the vocational staff and took courses at ——— University.

b: Yes, a counseling, teaching and professional certificate. An M.A. is minimal in addition to teaching.

Int:[4] Does the state have any special requirements?

Sub: No, the state does not require an advanced degree for teacher-counseling, but you must have been a successful teacher.

Int: How is this determined?

Sub: By the records at the school.

CASE 3:

a: (Laughs) I don't know . . .

Int: How's that?

Sub: Ever since I was an undergraduate . . . we didn't have these opportunities. In some respects this was a need I had, to see one person about college. My parents didn't know anything . . . so I was sensitive to the need to have someone to talk to. . . . I always had an interest in psychology. After the service, I had the GI Bill and I decided to take graduate work. I talked with a former teacher and he said the thing coming along the horizon was counseling. I took their graduate program—a year of occupational and vocational information, introduction to counseling, theory and practicum, mental hygiene. I had to have psychology courses, and a few education courses which I thought was ridiculous. I would rather have had abnormal psychology, but at this level, we don't need that.

Int: Is the practicum like an internship?

Sub: Yes—taped interviews, and we sat with the professor and criticized the interviews.

b: I think they really do have now. I think they want a master's.

Int: Does everyone have a master's degree?

Sub: No, we have a few left over from the old program—probably 95 per cent have some training . . . I really couldn't say. Every year

---

[4] *Int.* refers to probes by interviewer. *Sub.* indicates subject's response to probe.

new persons are introduced and Mr. ―――― [Principal] says that they have a degree in counseling.

Int: Are there any other requirements?

Sub: I think here they want undergraduate work in the teaching area. They prefer to have someone who has done some teaching first, who might be willing to take a course or two. I think teachers are happier when they think that the counselor has classroom experience and understands their problems.

c: My program at ―――― [university] was a very satisfactory program for what I engage in here. I think to do a really good job, I want to share some of the case load with the social worker. I would be far happier and more efficient in my work if I had clinical psychology and abnormal.

Int: Do you feel that your training limits your ability to deal with the problems you have?

Sub: My training has been quite adequate for those we have been talking about. If I had clinical training, I wouldn't have to refer cases so fast. But if I got that kind of training, I would want something better.

CASE 4:

a: I taught for a number of years. When a position was vacated—director of ―――― it was offered to me, but I didn't think I wanted it. But I was told that I had to take it. And I enjoyed it. I didn't have any graduate training. Then I was offered ―――― [an administrative job] and I took it. I got a degree in student personnel and went to State Teachers College. Then I went into a high school as assistant principal in guidance. I did more graduate work in counseling and took an internship for a [state] certificate. Then my husband and I moved to this area, and I took a job here.

b: A master's degree in counseling. Mine is in student personnel. Counseling techniques, diagnosis. Counselors must have been teachers.

c: Teaching experience is good. I think a counselor ought to be a psychologist, have a degree in counseling psychology.

Our materials suggest that counselors originate as teachers, especially the older ones, although the younger counselors are more likely to be in counseling full time and have little teaching experience. The younger counselors indicated that teachers tend to resent their presence on the assumption that younger counselors do not know enough about the problems of teaching. Teacher-counselors implied that counseling duties enabled them to become socially mobile within the school and that their chances of moving up or transferring to another school were increased. The illustrative materials presented reflect the interest of the two Lakeshore High counselors in obtaining training in psychology. This interest was expressed by many of the other counseling personnel at Lakeshore High, particularly by counselor-teachers and counselors. Their interest in such training is apparently related to two major professional concerns: (1) to enable them to deal with more involved student problems and thereby avoid referring students to social workers, and (2) to broaden their background in psychology so that more diagnostic tools and formal counseling techniques are available to them when they deal with students.

Over-all, the three questions did not produce responses that revealed as much concern with professionalization or competition with other personnel, such as social workers or psychologists, as we had expected. Our questions on routine activities, however, tended to elicit more information on this aspect of counseling. We shall discuss their responses below.

THE ORGANIZATION OF COUNSELING ACTIVITIES

Counseling activities at smaller schools are usually informal. The contacts of the counseling personnel with students, teachers, administrators, and others on the counseling staff are casual and may occur on the athletic field, in the halls, in classrooms, in the cafeteria, and the like. Although such contacts occur in similar fashion in larger schools (including Lakeshore High), increase in the scale of organization leads to formalized practices of referral and processing of students. In smaller schools where counseling is often a part-time position, counseling activities such as testing, checking student performance against ability, discipline, and advising students on college programs and future plans generally involve close teacher participation and cooperation. To explore the implications of the scale of organization for student-counselor relations, we asked a series of questions. Our first question was:

d: How do students come to your attention?

The responses of the two cases from the outside sample were as follows:

CASE 1:

 d: I would say about 50 per cent by referral from teachers. By this I mean that the teacher has contacted us and we call the student in.
  Int: And the other 50 per cent?
  Sub: Twenty-five per cent by parental contact.
  Int: When do students come in because of parental contact?
  Sub: Because of grades or study habits. Twenty-five per cent come in on their own.

CASE 2:

 d: Teacher referrals—referrals on breach of discipline. Also I send for students who have not been referred. I refer [them to] the services we can offer them in the guidance program. I explain what the battery for placement tests is. On the basis of these, we put them in homogeneous groups. We use them and the differential aptitude tests. This can help them get a better understanding of themselves.
  Int: How do students register for courses?
  Sub: The educational program is handled through the advisors. If they run into a snag, they see me.
  Int: Who are the advisors?
  Sub: The classroom teachers.
  Int: When do they get in touch with you?
  Sub: If a student insists that he wants to take a certain course, and the teacher will send him to me.
  Int: How do you decide this?
  Sub: On the basis of his tests and his past performance. If we don't think he can handle the work, we schedule another course.

The two cases from the outside sample reflect the influence of the teacher on the process by which students come to the attention of the counseling personnel. The teacher in smaller schools spots students who present problems in classroom and other school activities, and if he decides that they are more than routine problems, he refers them for counseling. When the scale of school organization increases, however, there is an emphasis upon professionally oriented full-time counseling, and the *routine* activities of programming courses, advising students on college and general vocational plans, etc., which were formerly performed by teachers are assigned to the counselor. At Lakeshore High School the counseling personnel are required to review the students' records periodically and to see them at least twice each year. The two cases from our Lakeshore High sample illustrate the routinization of student-counselor contacts:

CASE 3:

d: Mainly through principal referral. He has a complaint, he refers them to us after dealing with discipline. And then from teachers. Except for my observations at the beginning of the year when I see each individual.

Int: Do you see them all?

Sub: Yes, but I have 222 counselees and so sometimes I run into the end of the year before I see them. I see some of them three or four times. Administration policy is to see each of them at least twice a year.

Int: What other ways do students come to your attention?

Sub: I should say parental calls—indicative of malfunctioning, shall we say? Teacher referrals—many different circumstances—cafeterias, halls, etc. If we have a social worker they might consult us because they think the case needs a man counselor. But this is seldom. Usually the referral is the other way. I can't think of the others. One other way—on occasion Mr. ——— [the truant officer] might let us know. Usually through the principal . . . Sometimes through Mr. ——— directly. Last year there were not so many parent calls, but this year there have been many more—they're more concerned as they approach the senior year.

Int: This year there were more? How many?

Sub: About 20.

Int: And last year?

Sub: Probably last year about 12, about half the number this year. I anticipate more when programming begins.

CASE 4:

d: Through my own interviews. I make notations and observations when I think they need help. Through the division office. Also through teachers—this is not as frequent as it should be.

Int: How do you mean it's not as frequent as it should be?

Sub: I guess it's because they don't know who the student's counselor is sometimes, and the newness of the counseling system. Also through the parents. But mostly through the interview system. We get to know them reasonably well, so that you can pinpoint the problems. We renew relations with students and check their growth and development. I've had many self-referrals—it's very gratifying. Sometimes I get them through other students, directly or indirectly. They may tell me that some students are in a "gang" or something like that, and I try to look into it. But usually students come through my own observation.

The social worker responded to the question concerning the referral process as follows:

CASE 5:

d: Several ways. One is the referral from the division principal directly. These include those that teachers told me about and that then goes through channels; no matter how they come they have to come with his signature. Of those I find myself, I still have to go through the division principal. Even [with] those that are self-referrals I still have to do one of the forms in triplicate. One is for the division principal, one for Miss ——— [chairman of special services] and one for my record.

Int: What other ways do students come to your attention?

Sub: Yes, no matter how they come, they go through the division. The guidance counselors send some. Mr. ——— [the principal] does.

Int: Do they all go through the division first?

Sub: No, I can see them first. Another thing is parent's permission.

Int: Do you have to have this?

Sub: You should, you should. It's implicit.

These materials suggest that a professionally oriented, bureaucratically organized counseling program like that of Lakeshore High is more likely to discover student problems of all kinds as a consequence of the routine student-counselor contacts initiated by the counseling personnel. Several counselors stated that many problems are revealed when students are asked to come in for the routine periodic checks on their course-work progress and their future educational and occupational goals. A rough content analysis of the interviews with the Lakeshore High and outside samples suggested that referrals arising from routine administrative activities (e.g., the issuing of progress reports, failure notices, or lists of students qualified for extracurricular activities), from parental contacts with the school, and from the counselor's own initiative are more frequently reported by counselors and counselor-teachers than by teacher-counselors.

The social worker's activities are more bureaucratized than those of the three types of counselors, and he is unlikely to have contact with students without some kind of prior referral. His access to the origins of the referral process is limited by the administrative procedures that control the allocation of his professional activities. Although this screening of the social worker's cases is a mark of his higher professional status, decisions concerning the referral of cases to him are made by other personnel, particularly counselors, on the basis of their own interpretations of student problems.

DIFFERENTIAL CONCEPTIONS OF STUDENT PROBLEMS

The degree of professional orientation among counseling personnel suggests that an important feature of organizational scale and a bureaucratized counseling system should be reflected in the way student problems are defined by personnel variously situated within the organization of the school. Our interview materials indicate that student problems may be identified in a wide range of situational contexts—from fortuitous hallway encounters or casual cafeteria gossip to the bureaucratically prescribed routine counselor interviews with students. In schools where the referral system is not formally organized, the school personnel are more likely to define student problems as "typical" rather than as a "case" that warrants specialized treatment. A student who fails a course may be regarded by his teachers as "lazy," and he may be so described to his parents and counselor when the occasion arises. A talk with the student may satisfy the counselor that the student is "worried about a girl friend" or that he is "having trouble at home" and the matter may be dismissed. On the other hand, a course failure in a school with a more professionalized counseling system should activate the counselor to arrange a conference with the teacher to discuss the student's over-all record and behavior, interview the student to inquire about any problems he might have, speak to his parents to enlist their cooperation, and consider the advisability of scheduling regular counseling sessions or referral to the social worker for more intensive therapy.

Our interest in the organization of counseling activities is centrally related to the problem of the differentiation of students within the high school. We were concerned particularly with how student problems are differentially identified and classified by counseling personnel at Lakeshore High and at the other schools represented in our outside sample. To explore the differential identification and classification of student problems, we asked the following questions:

> *e:* What kinds of students do you come into contact with from day to day?
> *f:* Which kinds of students do you see the most?

CASE 1:

> *e:* The better student, I would say. Another range of 25 per cent will contact us because they are mainly interested in vocational information. And I have only a few who at the present time actually come in for some personal problem. Let me explain this. As the guidance department has been set up only for one semester, consequently we have had office hours only for one semester. It's more of a point to *want* to come in with their intimate and personal problems—this we know they have. I should qualify this. We feel we have built up a rapport with our students, but you can't satisfy everyone all the time. It will take time for them to know this thing is there for their use. It's the same as a doctor. He hangs up his shingle, but he knows that all who need him don't come in.
>
> *Int:* You say you know they have personal problems. How do you know this?
>
> *Sub:* Well, I think we can all recognize if we look back at our own high school career, I know I do, that I wish I could have talked to someone. We have statistics that students have problems, yet they have a reluctance to discuss them with adults. With their peers, it's a different thing because they have the same problems.
>
> *Int:* Are there any other students that you come in contact with from day to day?
>
> *Sub:* We have referrals by teachers.
>
> *Int:* When would a teacher refer a student to you?
>
> *Sub:* Most of them as being discipline combined with poor achievement.
>
> *Int:* How does the teacher decide this?
>
> *Sub:* By grades. Then we have referrals by the principal. Many times they are brought to the attention of the principal by the teacher for discipline and he speaks to them.
>
> *Int:* What are some of the things the students do?

Sub: They're antagonistic with intent to distract the teacher. Many times it's a personality conflict—two can't get along.

Int: What would a student do that would lead a teacher to think this?

Sub: Well, we had one situation where the teacher was not prepared. The first six weeks, he was all right. After six weeks he had run out of gas. After this he began to make comments about the facial expressions of a student. He was using this as ridicule. In this situation, he had superior students, and when they found they could get around him, they pushed him. Also, if a teacher has high standards, the students will rebel here. They feel they don't need to learn English, etc., "I'm not going to college," so will look out of the window. In this same line, we have some who are underachievers—not up to motivation. These stem from the family and cultural background by far. We have a growing population. Our school population is made up of about 25 per cent who have moved into our area from the hills of Kentucky. The aspirations of these people are practically nil. The parents don't work and they breed like rabbits.

Int: How do you decide that a student is an underachiever?

Sub: We give to our students the SCAT and we get the scores. We get a pretty good idea of what their potential could be. And by comparison, if he is in the 90th percentile, he is an underachieving individual regardless of what his motivation is. For example, one student got a *B* and he told the teacher he wanted a *C*. I asked him why and the student said, "the rest of the kids will make fun of me—will say I'm a brain."

Int: What did the teacher do?

Sub: Gave him a *B*. I know, because I did it. The situation happened to me, but other teachers have related the same thing.

Int: Did you talk to the boy?

Sub: Yes, he said he had maintained his status quo with the students and didn't want to change it. I told him he had earned it. If I had been a progressive education teacher, I would have given him a *C*.

f: [The question was phrased as follows:] Of the students we discussed a few moments ago, that is, the kinds of students that you come into contact with from day to day, which kinds do you see the most?

Sub: I see the average ability student who has been pressured by the teacher to do better. The student who is underachieving.

Int: What do you mean by an underachiever?

Sub: He is underachieving and getting into difficulty in the classroom.

Int: What do you mean, getting into difficulty?

Sub: They're discipline problems.

Int: Would you go into a little more detail?

Sub: For instance, a student who could do *C* or *C*-plus work was failing and failing due to the fact he had lost out. The teacher was ahead of him. He could not do his work. He found he had lost interest when he was behind and he thought he could not catch up.

CASE 2:

   e: Breach of discipline.
   f: Discipline cases.
      Int: What do you mean by discipline cases?
      Sub: Oh, lack of attention in the classroom. The teacher forgets that the student does not have a long attention span.

Although the first case reveals the organizational network for "catching" students with "problems," it is clear from the interview materials that a clinical orientation is not present. Even though family and cultural background are mentioned as a cause of underachievement, continued probing reveals that clinical imputations are lacking and such problems are linked to classroom conduct difficulties, but there is no reference to "underlying" or "deep-seated" conflicts involving the student as a person or his family. Both cases from our outside sample describe student problems in much the same way we would expect the man in the street to account for them. What may be discipline problems in everyday life can be viewed as acts of hostility or "deeper" problems for someone with a clinical perspective. The impression we obtain from our outside sample is one that may be described as a preclinical setting. The organizational structure is geared to handling and identifying "deeper" problems, but the trained personnel and vocabulary are absent.

The Lakeshore High personnel responded as follows:

CASE 3:

   e: Kinds? Probably 60 per cent are academic difficulties and in vocational areas. Thirty to 35 per cent have personal problems—they're left out of activities, not getting along with others, feelings about teachers. Five to 10 per cent I observe some serious problems—of course, these are the ones I would refer.
      Int: Refer?
      Sub: To the social worker.
   f: Academic and vocational. They want to know the number of credits they need for graduation, they have conflicts in programs, want lighter or heavier loads, problems of course selection in high school, ability

and interest, grades, study habits, low academic achievement, mis-understanding of teachers—this is related to the second type—what college area to go into, what courses are best for major area, career choice—many are not decided. Personal problems—lack of fitting in socially, behavior within group, lack of feeling of self-worth, may be small physically . . . not many of these, they don't like to admit this. How to communicate with parents and siblings, getting along with them. Lack of understanding—that's the major one, though—not having the chance to communicate, and not being understood, not making a team or a club—academic problems are related here, too, for student's personal problems. The serious problems: if I feel that a student is terribly underachieving—and we use that word a lot—and tests may not be testing. This may be the basis for automatic referral. But we try to get to the bottom of it, but students may be non-communicative. Then I refer him to the social worker as noncom-municative, hostile—for example, one who thought others were plotting against him, extremely nervous, and he'd break down and cry. These cases should be referred to the social worker, and she has a chance to refer them to a psychologist who is not in the school but works in the community. Once in a great while, I have a student who does not see the situation realistically in school, home, etc. They say, why work, plan, strive to be this or that. One or two students say, "What's it for?" They've had misfortunes, with indications of confusion and trouble. Five per cent is too high. Five per cent is too high [this statement was repeated]—it should be cut down. [This figure refers to his earlier statement that about 5 to 10 per cent of the students have serious problems.]

Int: Are there differences in the ways these types come to you?

Sub: No, only two ways: I get a note from the teacher, and by note from the division principal, or he might give me a phone call. Or I might look in at the homeroom and observe the kid, call his parents and talk to them as well as to the student. And, of course, through the student himself. I've had more this year than last—it fits the pattern of parents calling more. Counseling is the most needed thing for adolescents, but it is so discouraging because there are so many other people that they fall back on, like friends, parents, siblings. As they get older, they're more sensitive to problems. They may feel inadequate earlier and begin to see things. When they're freshmen, you can see things that are so obvious.

Int: Obvious?

Sub: The kid who never contributes anything, not participating, a loner, or overly aggressive—the extremes are noticeable.

Int: And you think these things come up later?

Sub: When they get older, they find it's been happening for two years now. "What am I doing?" they say. But the kid may put off coming for counseling—it's too threatening.

Int: Do many come in voluntarily?

Sub: This year it's been increasing, but usually you have to seek them out. This year 4 to 8 kids have come in. But what can you do if you call them in? You have to be careful, and if we have the four-year program [i.e., students are assigned the same counselor for four years] we can give them the benefit of the doubt. But the social worker may interpret from the start.

CASE 4:

e: You mean, what is the nature of their problems? All kinds. The majority are those having academic problems. I probably seek them out—I go over their grades at marking period. I seek out those who don't do as we think they should. There are about 10 or 15 students with continuing problems—for example, a father has died, there's a split home, not being able to accept responsibility. I have a full quota of fully disorganized students—those that need help. They're not necessarily psychological problems—they can't get things done. But the bulk of cases are academic—a lack of knowing how to study, lack of accepting demands of classes, or personal problems that prevent them from applying themselves. I also have students who have to drop a class, or revise their plans, students getting anxious about educational and vocational plans.

f: Underachievers—they are prevalent with the increase in standards. Many lack the maturity to reach standards. Many don't believe in their own ability—they're not as competitive as they might be. I shouldn't say that—they lack confidence. They're satisfied with passing grades, they're not realistic about grades at the six-week marking period. The new students are more oriented to the higher standards.

Int: Are those with personal problems a different type?

Sub: There are very few with personal problems who are achieving. Personal problems are the obvious ones—split homes, overindulgences, lack of maturity, lack of self-appraisal. Also, you have to work a great deal with them; you have to wait for maturity. I try to work in as nonthreatening a way as possible.

Int: Do you pick up these students in the same way?

Sub: Pretty much—identifying them in the initial interview—unless they show up in their overt behavior. I offer them counseling service. This year they have been more receptive to the service, more realistic.

CASE 5:

e: These vary. One is quite frequent—underachievement. At least it's labeled as such. It isn't always that. Parents often think it is and will not always accept the results of our guidance counselor. They want the child to go to college, say Harvard or Princeton. In some cases, a kid who can achieve doesn't achieve because he wants to hurt the parents. Then there is the acting out, aggressive youngster. I see a lot of boys this way.

Int: What do they do?

Sub: They consistently create trouble in class, such as talking aloud and being defiant to the teacher. Quick to respond to any signs of disapproval from the teacher. These kids often have trouble in gym.

Int: Why is that?

Sub: This is a place to really assert yourself aggressively. Another reason is there is probably some latent homosexuality in the gym teachers who go along with this. There are those who are thought to be effeminate.

Int: Who might say this?

Sub: The division principal might.

Int: Does it come from others, too?

Sub: Yes.

Int: Who are they?

Sub: I really don't know. These kids, say in gym, who sit around in a short period and talk about creative things, about things like ——— Street [known locally to be a bohemian area of the nearby city], the ——— [a hang-out of so-called "beats"], things that are unusual. The gym teacher will go over and ask them why they talk so effeminately. I get another type. Somebody involved in a racial mix-up. It's reflected by the school, which says the parents worry about the Negro boys who get interested in white girls who give them attention. These are usually intelligent kids on both sides. The girls (white) are usually not as attractive, wear glasses, have braces on their teeth. For the Negroes braces are considered a sign of prestige.

Int: Does this sort of thing develop into anything?

Sub: Into marriage? Not usually. This is one way girls who are not attractive can hurt father. It is one way for the Negro boy to enhance his ego. For the Negro it is a pressure to strive for middle-class things. Then there is the kid who resists school altogether. He can't perform in school at all. The family is usually a professional family. He's always failing, yet there's no apparent why. Well, that's about it.

f: I get the impression that I see underachievers the most, if one can use this term. This is the biggest emphasis here [at Lakeshore High].

Int: Could you elaborate?

Sub: It's somebody, who in the estimation of parents, teachers, counselors, that he isn't measuring up to his potential. One is the feelings of the parents that a kid is not achieving. Two, the division principal's feelings based on the results of our entrance examinations.

The detailed accounts given by these cases from the Lakeshore High School sample are interesting not only because their content provides examples of the kinds of interpretations that are made about student problems, but also because the extensive spontaneous remarks, which were characteristic of this group, underline how a more professional perspective produces *more* problems and how a clinical orientation dominates the descriptive terms used. The continual reference to academic problems by the more professionally oriented counseling personnel is not the same kind of reference used by teacher-counselors. For the former group academic problems are merely signs of deeper underlying emotional or personality difficulties whose roots are to be found in parent-child relations or, when the personality is viewed as disturbed, in student-student or student-teacher relationships. Terms like "obsessive-compulsive," "dependent-independent," "aggressive," "hostile," and the like are routinely used by the professionally oriented personnel whose primary duties are devoted to counseling students.

The extraction of "deeper" problems. Two points are suggested by our materials: (1) The professionally oriented counselor will seek out students who are thought to have problems, and whatever problems are mentioned as manifestly the reason for the contact (and regardless of who initiated the contact), there is always an attempt to probe (or to refer students to someone like the social worker for probing) what are believed to be "deeper" underlying problems of psychodynamic origin. (2) The underachiever is probably the central preoccupation of counselor-teachers and counselors, and the achievement problems are invariably viewed as having "deeper" roots. The professionally oriented counselor with a clinical perspective tends to view the underachiever not merely as someone who has talent that is being wasted and who therefore needs "help," but also as a "case" of parental pressure, disorganized family, unrealistic aspirations, and the like.

This tendency is significantly related to the ways in which clinical conceptions of student problems, bureaucratically integrated into a system for differentiating the student population, may alter the student's and parents' conceptions of themselves, of each other, and of "what is best" for the student academically, socially, and emotionally, i.e., psychodynamically. Thus, it is not that the so-called "class-ascribed" character of student and parent aspirations are irrelevant for the outcome of the student's high school career. Rather, the implementation of college-going aspirations is made problematic by the ways in which they are interpreted and re-interpreted by professionals in a bureaucratically organized system.

We shall explore this organizational process in greater detail by presenting the responses of those interviewed to questions that were designed to reveal the kinds of criteria used by counseling personnel for classifying student problems. These questions were phrased as follows:

> *g:* Would you tell me about the most recent case that you had that was of X type (or X types)?[5]
> *h:* Who referred this student to you?
> *i:* What did the student do that led to the referral?

Our two outside cases responded as follows:

CASE 1:

> *g:* I can think of one who ranked in the 90th percentile in ability tests and ranked from around the 70th to the 80th percentile in the ITED, and his grade-point average when he finished the school year was about a D. In this situation, he is a "low-aspiration" student.
>
> *Int:* How do you decide this?
>
> *Sub:* Oh, by interview, trying to find out what he wanted to do when he got out of school. He said he did not care what he wanted to do just so long as he made enough money to get beer and whiskey and have a good time with the girls.
>
> *h:* He was in my class. I asked him to come in.
>
> *i:* He was failing.
>
> *Int:* What did he do in class?
>
> *Sub:* As little work as possible.

5 X type (or X types) refers to the interviewee's response to question *f* presented above.

CASE 2:

g: There was a boy that was sent by a teacher because of lack of attention to the discussion. It was a culmination of instances. His attention was getting worse and worse. Her perception was good and she sent him in. It was a breakdown of about four weeks prior to the referral. His work was slovenly.

   Int: What do you mean when you say the "teacher's perception was good"?

   Sub: That she noticed that his attention was getting worse and she sent him in.

h: The teacher.

i: He was day-dreaming when the teacher was discussing material. She called on him and he didn't answer.

CASE 3:

g: Very high I.Q.—140. He didn't want any help from adults, didn't want responsibility. It was about two weeks ago, and I referred him to the social worker. He said things that didn't sound like a healthy kid, like "I get so sick of myself, usually after marking period." Then the other kind—low ability, but overachieving like mad. Parents want him to do better. Then the middle group who are trying to get through, get tutors.

h: [Question was rephrased: How did you pick up the 140 I.Q. case?] I picked him up by grade report—it was a glaring extreme.

   Int: What did you do?

   Sub: I made an appointment and presented him with this.

   Int: What did he do at the first contact?

   Sub: He just sat in the chair. I asked him what's new this year?

   Int: How did you perceive how he felt about being called in?

   Sub: I reflected the way he sat—"You don't want to have anything to do with adults." "No. They're all right, I know you have a job to do." I asked him if it was all right to make an appointment—would that be O.K.? He said "Yeah, that's all right." The next time he expressed some of these things. I told him about the school's job. [The interviewee then made a lengthy aside in the course of which he said, "So many teachers have to wear so many hats. Teachers as well as counselors." He mentioned some incident about some girls who had reported that a boy was masturbating. They went to see the counselor, and the counselor went to see the teacher. The interviewee then returned to the case of the boy with the 140 I.Q.] The next time he came I felt he was uncommunicative.

   Int: What happens if you refer a kid and he doesn't want to be referred?

Sub: We have to contact his parents . . . no, the principal may order him to see the social worker.

Int: Would you maintain the relationship with the student?

Sub: I think the principal would want me to continue. If the social worker has a good relationship [with the student]. I feel that we shouldn't have to do the paper-work such as programming. [This statement was in reference to a case where he said that the student was working with a social worker, but the social worker sent the student to him (the counselor) for programming.]

i: [Queston was answered in response to *h* above and so was not asked.]

CASE 4:

g: Yes, a Negro boy with an I.Q. of 125. We try to identify them early because they often have inadequate drives; they're easily discouraged.

Int: Are you seeing him now?

Sub: Periodically, almost always at his request. He was doing way below average work—he repeated algebra. He has more interest this year. He came in to ask about college—he asked whether I really meant it that scholarships were available. He's proud of his accomplishment, although he's not achieving much above 3. He's trying hard.

Int: Did you pick him up as a freshman?

Sub: Partly at the initial interview—his first grades were 5's—it was part of the routine interviews.

Int: Is he now a sophomore?

Sub: Yes, and our relationship has improved—he would like to go into law.

Int: How do you mean the relationship has improved?

Sub: He comes in voluntarily, talks frankly, he says he didn't work as hard as he could, he analyzes his own difficulties, he responds to making out his program schedule.

Int: Is he planning a college career?

Sub: He says, "I'd like to be a lawyer, but I don't think I can be." He has a low aspiration level. He's a refined boy, a good home.

Int: Have you seen his family?

Sub: No, and that's interesting. They are always going to come in but they never do. I've offered to see them on Saturday or in an evening, but they never came.

Int: Would you tell me about the most recent case that you had that was a personal problem type?[6]

6 In our interviews we asked for "the most recent case" of each of the types of problems mentioned in the responses of interviewees to question *f*. The response of Case 4 to this line of questioning illustrates the detailed information that counselors may obtain about their student clients.

Sub: One girl—her father is a professional man. Her parents have been separated some years. She's the eldest daughter. Her mother has remarried and her children feel she married below their cultural level. The girl lives with her mother and she [the girl] is antagonistic and can't stand her stepfather. Her father is a busy man—he promises her things but doesn't follow through. The girl is dating university boys—she uses lying devices with her mother. They're at an impasse—she resists her mother. At the last marking period, she failed all her subjects. She said she did this deliberately—she's a very bright girl. Her mother called in after the holiday. She said that the girl's father is going to put her in a private school, but her grades are poor, so we made plans to get her grades up. I talked with her teachers, and they were happy to have her go. The girl became dependent on me. Her mother wanted to have an after-school arrangement where she stays after school to study. I told her I didn't play that role. Her mother arranged for a tutor. Now the girl has decided that she doesn't want to go to a private school . . . she's backsliding to where she used to be.

Int: Has her mother contacted you?

Sub: Yes, I get different stories from the girl and her mother. I believe the mother is honest and interested—sincere. I think the home situation is not good, but the stepfather tends to stay out of the father role. Mother has come to see me at the parent-teachers and other activities so I think she's interested. The girl's father is irresponsible. The mother says that the girl feels she doesn't have what her friends have. The best thing would be to get into contact with her father, but I hesitate. The relationship is getting tense—the girl is trying me against her mother's decisions. She called on Saturday night about a dating fracas. I'm concerned—her mother says that the girl is dishonest—I feel she [the girl] feels I might be another person to use.

Int: How did you come to see her? What brought her in?

Sub: Again, lack of achievement. I don't think there was a crucial issue. Her I.Q. is 128.

Int: Was she called into the office on grades?

Sub: Yes. On her first contact, she had an "I don't care" attitude. Her friends were terribly important to her. It is a good crowd in the higher social bracket. She tries to keep up with them. They keep up their good grades and school activities, but the girl is too involved to get recognition, too emotionally involved. Her teachers are very concerned—she seems to disintegrate when work has to be handed in.

Int: Did you call her mother?

Sub: I called her for an interview.

Int: How was she in the first conference?

Sub: Very nice and honest. She told me what I knew—that she was maintaining a larger house than they can afford for the girl.

Int: Did you say the girl was back where she was before?

Sub: Oh, I should say that usually I refer these cases to the social worker. I did the first of this year, but both because of the social worker's case load and the girl's reaction to the social worker—she said, "I hated her so that I cut class and haven't done any studying since"— I've been counseling her. I don't think it's a deep-seated difficulty— environmental rather than psychological.

Int: Are there any other types of students that you see?

Sub: There are many who are getting along—they are more usual— I see them about long-range goals, future education, vocational information, to talk about activities.

Int: Would you tell me about the last case you saw which was of this type?

Sub: I see them during the study period. This means that some get more attention than others. Five boys—not delinquents—but problems. They have a lingo, they take skill classes.

Int: What's that?

Sub: Lower level, "opportunity" students, lowest section. Most of them are graded 6, which is actually failing, but if the student is not academic, they are given 6 and passed. One of these boys—his mother is concerned about his grades, she won't accept the boy's limitations— the boy came in to see me about college. I saw the boys in group sessions. I attempted to study their vocational goals, their aims and ideas, get them to see them more realistically. One of them was interested in auto mechanics. I told him he didn't have to go to college for that. I gave them a booklet called "If you're not going to college." First I just let them talk—they talked like big shots.

Int: What did they talk about?

Sub: Cars, a lot. One boy's father has a Cadillac—they talked about speed, etc. I asked them for their help. One of the teachers was doing research on teen-age lingo and I asked them if they would tell me about it. Another time, I posed a problem: If a boy had stolen or borrowed a car and picked them up, and then they were caught, what would they do? [She stated the further condition that they didn't know it was stolen—"They knew what I was talking about," she said.] Most of them agreed that they would pass the buck—they knew about the law, about first offenses—they quoted the law. I established good relations with them—I gave them homework, asked for their help in discussing what are values and how to set goals. They seem to respond.

Int: Have any of their mothers called?

Sub: One of the boys' mothers, a widow, called. She's trying hard. She has two boys, the other is not a good student but he's doing well. She's concerned about this one. I think the mother is a dull person. When I say to her that we must plan for a non-college program, she says he must go to college. She's concerned because he doesn't bring homework home.

Int: How does the boy behave?

Sub: He's loud—typical behavior—smarty, everything is funny. The teachers think he's disrespectful.

Int: Is the attendance at the counseling group voluntary?

Sub: Yes.

Int: How does the mother feel about it?

Sub: I haven't discussed it with her. We haven't talked about their families. Their homes are reasonably good, the parents are interested. The mothers work. All are laborers.

CASE 5:

g: A young man, 16, a junior. He's capable and has shown spurts of getting 1's and 2's. Prominent parents, stepfather. The stepfather has been married twice, the mother three times. Material well-being, the kid drives a convertible to school. He's a sad-looking boy. He doesn't feel he's attractive to girls. He has incorporated the parents' Republican interests and he champions this. He wants to be a doctor. [The interviewer informed the interviewee, a social worker, that the boy's counselor had mentioned this case. The social worker said that the counselor exaggerates, that the boy's absence is due to illness and that he is not as bad as the counselor says he is.]

Int: Have you ever talked to his parents?

Sub: Oh, yes, many times. The mother is very active with club work. He's very attached to his mother.

h: I believe Mr. —— [principal] did or she [the counselor] might have.

i: I think probably tardiness. He was always getting here late in the morning.

These materials illustrate the range of perspectives and depth of counseling activities that are activated by the identification of student problems. Of the two outside cases presented, Case 2 is more representative of the interviews in this sample. The "lack of attention" that was the occasion for the referral of the student mentioned by Case 2 was not described or interpreted in other than everyday terminology—"his attention was getting worse and worse . . . his work was slovenly." (We should note that the more professionalized Case 4, a counselor, describes the behavior of one of the boys in the group session in similar terms—"he's loud—typical behavior—smarty, everything is funny." It may be significant that this boy was an "opportunity" student from what the counselor considered to be a laboring family, and one she thought was not college material.) All the "outside" counseling personnel had come from the ranks of the teaching staff, were generally older than those at Lakeshore High, and were not products of graduate programs of guidance and counseling. They rarely used clinical terminology, and their vocabulary and social-type characterizations of students were similar to what we might expect persons in everyday life to use, such as students with "poor" home life, "teen-age" problems, "spoiled" kids, and the like. In this regard, it is interesting to note that our interviews with teacher-counselors at Lakeshore High School reveal that they described students in almost identical terms.[7]

The language used by the Lakeshore High cases reflect the more professional training that is characteristic of this counseling staff. There is not only a tendency to use the clinical terminology and mode of analysis—"uncommunicative," "emotionally involved," "inadequate drives," "she is trying me against her mother's decision," etc.—there is also a self-conscious concern about the methods of counseling. Case 3 "reflected the way he sat" following the Rogerian technique, and Case 4 states that "our relationship has improved" and declines to "play a role" vis-à-vis a student.

Comments similar to those made by Case 3 that members of the school personnel have to "wear so many hats" and his complaint that counselors should not be required to do the clerical work for social workers were also expressed by others in the Lakeshore High sample. Such comments indicate a concern for more explicit division of counseling functions and recognition of the legitimacy of the professional status of counselors vis-à-vis social workers. The

---

[7] Nine of the counseling personnel at Lakeshore High School were full-time counselors, 5 were counselor-teachers, and 7 were teacher-counselors. The teacher-counselors all regarded themselves as teachers who would resume full-time teaching as soon as enough new counselors with master's degrees in guidance and counseling were appointed.

social worker's dismissal of the counselor's opinions of the student discussed in Case 5 reflects the conflict structured by the differential status accorded these two groups within the organization. The more professional aspect of the conflict is illustrated by the remarks of Case 4. This counselor says of a student who has returned to her, saying that she hated the social worker, that "I don't think it's a deep-seated difficulty—environmental rather than psychological." The reference to the "environmental" basis of the difficulty appears to be offered by this counselor to define the student's problems as "surface" in character, and thus legitimize the resumption of counseling with the student.

Case 4 also illustrates the counselor's potential influence on student aspirations and plans. She reports counseling boys who were not viewed as qualified for college to help them "study their vocational goals, their aims and ideas . . . get them to see them more realistically." Such counseling is often extended also to their parents, who, as one counselor put it, must be "cooled out" to revise their high and unrealistic aspirations for their children. At Lakeshore High where parents are strongly college-oriented, this is a typical counseling problem.

The social worker's (Case 5) reference to a recent "underachiever" presumably began as a routine problem of tardiness. The brief excerpt that presents his responses to these questions does not reveal the extensive clinical imputations made about this student by the social worker. Further details about this case will appear below, where we pursue the processing of the recent cases within the organization up to the time of the interview. Additional questions were asked about the recent cases in an attempt to pinpoint the counseling personnel's conceptions and classifications of problems and their ways of handling them. Our interview probes were directed by our interest in the question: Would the cases mentioned by the professionally trained and oriented counseling staff at Lakeshore High have been considered problems had they appeared in a high school with a less professionalized and bureaucratized counseling system? Our assumption has been that they would not be given much attention because the organization of the counseling system is the crucial selective factor for "drawing out" the problems from students. We assume that any student who is questioned by a counselor about some "problem" will always be able to offer some "reason" to explain it, particularly if he is pressed for one and if the counselor makes comments that suggest the nature of the responses the student might make. Our impression is that, like many adolescents who come into contact with the law, students confronted by a counselor's attempts to "get at the problem" have become aware of the importance of having a problem to explain their lack of achievement or behavioral misconduct. Thus, the bureaucratized and professionalized counseling system may provide adolescents with the motivations, the labels, and the justifications for a wide range of "problems."

The following questions were designed to reveal more about the flow of information concerning the recent cases and the framework within which problems come to be identified and classified:

j: What did you think was the problem?
k: How did you handle the problem?
l: What kinds of information did you have about the student before he came to see you? What was the source of the information?

CASE 1:

j: I have a feeling the problem in this situation was principally family background. His mother and father were separated. His father was remarried. His father would not give him money. So the youngster went to live with a friend's family.

k: The interview came about because of the STS program and we discussed what he was going to do.

Int: What happened?

Sub: He said that he didn't care. Just what I had told you previously.

l: I had him as a student—the cumulative record. This includes his grades from the first grades clear through his high school career. We have a general idea of family income and home conditions. We have the number of brothers and sisters, absentee and truancy records.

Int: How do you get the information about the family?

Sub: Through interview.

Int: Do you contact the parents?

Sub: No, we get the information from the counselee. They're pretty truthful.

CASE 2:

> *j:* I never think of a cause. I don't try to postulate reasons until I have all the information. I did not formulate a conclusion.
>
> *k:* I gave him some tests. The Wechsler-Bellevue, which was low in verbal intelligence and average on performance scale; the Iowa Skills Battery—grade placement was low on reading and language. The differential aptitude battery was low on abstract.
>
> *Int:* What did you do then?
>
> *Sub:* Well, the following day the civics teacher caught him with some pornographic literature. He was referred to the police for this. I spoke to —— [the boy] about the pornographic literature.
>
> *Int:* What did you say? [At this point the interviewer noticed the interviewee hesitating because of her sex. The interviewer then said: "Look at me as a scientist."]
>
> *Sub:* Well, the pictures were pretty bad. I told him that sex was the natural law in the marital state. Otherwise, it had adverse affects. It could lead to ultimate perversion.
>
> *Int:* Did the student say anything?
>
> *Sub:* No, his reaction was submissive and he agreed with me. You see the technique I use is a jovial manner—and the students like it. You know they call me "baldy" and "fatso." They say they'd rather take anything than go to see me because I'm too nice.
>
> *l:* What the teacher said about the four-week period of inattention. His record card which showed the Terman-McNemar Intelligence test given in the seventh grade and the Iowa tests of Basic Skills, multi-level edition, given in the eighth grade.
>
> *Int:* What did the tests show?
>
> *Sub:* I really don't recall exactly, but it was low.

The significant feature of both these illustrative cases lies in the common-sense interpretations placed upon the students' problems. The two principal types of problems—disciplinary and poor academic performance—are described with the same kinds of conceptions one would expect from the man on the street. In these cases and others in the outside sample, the students' "run-ins" with teachers, other students, and administrators are viewed as commonplace occurrences, and if they are considered problems at all, they are explained by "poor upbringing," a "mean streak," a "sassy, spoiled brat," and the like. And when students are considered to have academic problems that can be resolved, the procedures used for handling such cases do not include references to personal or family problems in clinical terms, but admonitions to "work harder," "listen to your mother," "stop playing around after school," etc. Case 2 presents an illustration of the form such an admonishment may take in the case of a conduct problem. There was a distinct absence of references by the interviewees in the outside sample to the need for treatment, personal counseling, or psychotherapy, or to "deep-seated problems" underlying the manifest conduct of students. Student problems were treated as they appeared to be—as obvious results of "poor home life," "bad manners," "status-conscious parents," and so on.

We would assume that the professionally oriented and trained counseling personnel would not accept such "obvious" explanations of student problems. Poor grades, casual complaints about situations at home, about studying, about the opposite sex or friends are *merely appearances*. A clinical orientation would search for the underlying causes of underachievement, peer problems, teacher-student conflicts, and the like. The bureaucratization of counseling in a professional (and clinical) direction should tend to integrate the organizational concern for identifying talent with the efforts of the counseling personnel to develop student capabilities through better personal, school, and home adjustment. Consider the following materials from our Lakeshore High sample:

CASE 3:

  j: I had no idea. I don't think it was a lack of training or lack of sophistication, but on the first contact, I think it would be jumping the gun. Here's a kid who was noncommunicative—to say more would be interpretive without basis.

  k: I had three meetings with him. I told him that if he wanted to talk to me at night, to call. He said, "Well, maybe."

    Int: How did he behave?

    Sub: He said, "I don't need any help. I know you're trying to do a job." Looking back now, I might have missed. I don't know whether I missed something. Maybe he was trying to test me, to see if I was really interested. He just said, "I don't need any help. Lots of them have tried to help me." So I don't know. Maybe if I had presented it differently . . .

  l: None at all. Then when I checked over his scores I found the discrepancy between ability and grades. Then I went to the personal files to see if there were any recent occurrences that might indicate that the student was fighting himself or society. I had a couple of teacher's notes before I saw him the first time. I would generally go to each teacher to see how he was getting along. But I didn't in this case because it was obvious that teachers couldn't tell me much about what was wrong with him. Case conferences are most vital—getting teachers together to discuss a student, to get information from all the teachers. Time-wise it's so difficult to get teachers together.

CASE 4:

j: Mainly that he was pretty limited. He was quite unattractive and loud. It was obvious that he would be a behavior problem.

Int: Was that the teacher's comment?

Sub: Yes, he was frequently out of class. I saw him individually once a week—I didn't get too far. He doesn't think he has a problem. He didn't have much to talk about. It's difficult with skills students.

Int: He doesn't think he has a problem?

Sub: No, he's not concerned about himself yet.

Int: Do you think as he grows older there will be more recognition of a problem?

Sub: I don't know. [She commented here that she did not know whether or not the student had manual dexterity—apparently referring to his interest in auto mechanics, and her counseling him toward that occupation.] I don't think he'll get disturbed about himself. All he wants is a good car, a good job, and a good home.

l: Test data, his folder, personal data from elementary through junior high school—it has his report cards. There are valuable teacher comments and parent responses. The junior high school sends a brief anecdotal account of the student and an evaluation. When they come here they fill out a personal information form—parents' education, parents' occupation, etc., what they have in common with mother and father, a self-evaluation check list. This is not too significant—they don't know what the words mean.

Int: Did you collect any information about the student on your own?

Sub: Yes, but I didn't do it systematically. There was the initial interview. I don't use the case-work approach—I feel I have enough information. The kids are used to interviews—I ask them how they are getting along, what problems they are having, sometimes about their family, although I have this information on the data folder. I don't want them to feel that I'm collecting information. Students who are social work cases in the junior high schools are carried here.

CASE 5:

j: I think the problem is a need to punish himself. And it's related to an Oedipal complex with three fathers. A conflict with the father over the mother. She's girlish and kinda cute. If you ask why does he do this, it's a means of avoiding success and thus a means of being compared with other men in the mother's life.

k: It's not completely handled. But, by a supportive relationship which consisted of helping him in difficult situations and helping to interpret why he was late. To see that he needs to function independently of his mother and parents. This also included work with the mother so that she sees that she had to respond in an understanding way rather than critically. He's competing with poppa all the time. Helping him with problems with girls. How to get them to keep trying. Giving him a father figure that's accepting.

l: From the counselor, from Mr. ——— [Division Principal], from the cumulative folder.

Int: What did it tell you?

Sub: It told me he was capable of grades and that he was not making them. That he was tardy and absent. It told me about his performance in school. There was a repetition in the teachers' statement that he didn't work with the class. I made some deductions. I felt he was trying to get to the attention of the school authorities. That he was considered a funny-looking character and his clothes. There was some question about his shoes—they were old and worn out. They are really nice people. The kid has been deprived because of so many changes, but the family is rather nice. They're very conscious of their position and not wanting to give you information about the family. I've had cases like this with colored kids.

The responses in Case 3 again reflect this counselor-teacher's concern about the professional aspect of his activities. In his responses to earlier questions, he had expressed a desire to "share some of the case load with the social worker" (see question *c*) as well as his dissatisfaction about being saddled with doing her clerical work. Here, the counselor-teacher expresses doubts about his handling of the case ("I might have missed. . . . Maybe he was trying to test me. . . . Maybe if I had presented it differently . . . ," etc.) His comments also illustrate how the investigation of problems may be directed toward seeking information that will document the notion that a problem does in fact exist ("I went to the personal files to see if there were any recent occurrences that might indicate that the student was fighting himself or society.")

The presumption on the part of many counseling personnel that students *do* have the problems imputed to them is clearly illustrated in the remarks of Case 4 that the student in question "doesn't think he has a problem." The comment that follows this statement— "He didn't have much to talk about. It's difficult with skills students"—and her judgment that "I don't think he'll get disturbed about himself. All he wants is a good car, a good job, and a good home" is perhaps too eloquent to require further comment here. It may well be that it is only those students who are noncommunicative to questions about "how they are getting along" and "what problems they are having" who have the option of remaining ignorant of the "problems" they have. When such problems are presumed by the social worker to be expressions of an "Oedipus complex," the "noncommunicative" response may be the student's only defense against the gratuitous efforts to "help" him gain a "better understanding" of himself.

Information-gathering by the counselor. Although the social workers tended always to be more clinically oriented in their descriptions of cases than the others, this orientation was also reflected in the responses of counselors and less professionalized members of the counseling staff. In order to inquire further into the currency of this view of student problems at Lakeshore High and the schools represented in the outside sample, we asked additional questions about how and from whom the counseling personnel sought information concerning the student, and about the nature of the discussion and information they obtained. The following questions were asked:

   m: Did you talk with anyone else at school about the case?
   n: (If "yes" to *m:*) Who were the persons you talked with? What are their positions at the school?
   o: What did you talk with him about?
   p: Did you talk with the student's parents about the case?
   q: What did you talk about?
   r: What was the last thing you had to do with the case?[8]

CASE 1:
   m: Yes, he came to the attention of the county prosecutor. He was

[8] Questions were not asked directly when answers to them were included in the interviewee's responses to previous questions.

charged with a felony, but it was not brought to trial—insufficient evidence.

Int: What was it all about?

Sub: Some little girl accused him of rape.

Int: Did you talk with anyone at school about the case?

Sub: The principal and the other counselor. We work together in this kind of situation. Otherwise we don't bother.

p: No, we didn't after we found out what the charge was. It was out of our hands.

Int: Did you talk with the parents in connection with the student's grades?

Sub: No.

Int: What did you do then?

Sub: Nothing, because the prosecuting attorney took over.

r: At the point when the prosecutor took over, we turned the case over to him.

Int: What was the last thing you heard about the case?

Sub: The last thing I heard, he was working in the fields pulling weeds out of the crops, working with the Mexicans.

Int: How old is he?

Sub: Seventeen. The prosecutor advised us the case was dropped because of insufficient evidence and he told us what the boy was doing.

CASE 2:

m: Yes, I spoke to the civics teacher because he was the one that caught him with the pornographic literature.

o: We talked about the fact that he had it and where he had gotten it.

p: No, the police did.

Int: What did you do then?

Sub: We switched him to another class in lower math and general civics.

Int: How did you decide to do that?

Sub: On the basis of the Wechsler-Bellevue.

r: I talked to the student. He was not very verbal. He was relieved to switch sections.

Int: What do you mean?

Sub: Well, he didn't say anything, and he just nodded his head.

Int: What was the last thing you heard about the case?

Sub: He passed both subjects with a *C* grade.

Int: From whom did you get the information?

Sub: From the teachers.

Int: Did you contact the teachers?

Sub: Yes.

CASE 3:

m: Yes.

n: I told the social worker about it. I told her I had a boy I wanted to refer to her, to prepare her for it, telling her it's a possibility. I mentioned it to the principal's secretary. I asked her if she had any experiences with the boy. She reported the same experiences—he was short, gruff.

Int: What did you find in his folder?

Sub: No behavioral things. But I found out from the physical education people that he went out for one sport, quit, then another and then quit. But as far as the folder goes, no discipline slips. Nothing in class.

Int: Have you observed him in class?

Sub: No, but in the homeroom I made a point to see him. He was quite peaceful and quiet—not obnoxious. I had a few communications with other kids in the class. He's a Jewish boy—his father is a medical laboratory technician. His personality evaluation is above average. In junior high school he got *C*'s and *D*'s in the seventh grade—he did better in the eighth. He had college aspirations in the eighth grade—he planned to go to M.I.T. Now he has none at all.

p: I made an appointment and had a meeting with his father. I had checked on the boy's grade, and I had an appointment made for a week. In the meantime, the father said how he felt. He said ever since ——— [the boy] had been in school, he's had trouble. He didn't want to study. The attitude of the father was that he was a busy person. He felt that there were many neglectful moments, throwing the entire responsibility on the school. It was a short appointment.

Int: Did the father come in before the boy?

Sub: Yes, sometimes if I miss [presumably failing to pick up the student for poor grades] parents call it to my attention. It was a short appointment. He was here for 25 minutes. He said the boy didn't have too many friends. I wish it could be explained away so simply.

Int: What did he think was the problem?

Sub: He had no idea. There is no indication of change. He said anything you can do, that he didn't know where to go. I told him that if it's a deep-rooted thing there is a possibility that I might refer him to the social worker. He said fine, that he couldn't communicate with him, that he has a negative attitude. He said "I can't suggest that he do anything because if I do, he'll do just the opposite."

Int: Did you say he tended to blame the school?

Sub: No, not at all—he said that the boy had good teachers, that they had tried to get next to ——— [the boy]. He didn't blame the school at all. He was searching himself for a few times. He said,

"Maybe I'm neglecting—when you think you're doing a job, you may be missing."

Int: Have you seen his mother?

Sub: No. He didn't suggest it. I'm sure that the social worker will make contact with her.

Int: How would you decide whether or not to call his mother?

Sub: If the father had made comments about the mother, like "Well, my wife won't let —— grow up." If he gave some indication—it would be best to get the two together.

  r: The last meeting I mentioned before. He didn't have much to say. I told him I was going to suggest that he might see someone. Nothing happened.

Int: Was he here the whole period?

Sub: No, when he was so negative, about a half-period and I let him go. I'll probably be calling you again in a week or so, I said. He said O.K.

CASE 4:

  m: Yes.

  n: I talked with the division principal about the group. He has let up on the disciplinary action since he was told about the group. [The counselor mentioned that when the boys get into trouble they talk about it in the group.]

Int: Do you make it a practice of talking about trouble in the group?

Sub: [The counselor said there was some controversy among the counselors about this—whether or not they should talk to counselees about the trouble they get into.] I don't scold them, but try to get them to reason.

Int: Did you talk to any other person about this case?

Sub: I talked to his teachers. The boy does read—his reading skills are fairly normal. I talked with his English teacher about a reading list for him. The teacher was upset about his behavior. She wasn't very cooperative, but she doesn't report him so much now.

Int: Has his behavior changed?

Sub: He does better—he's more embarrassed.

Int: About being loud? How does the teacher feel?

Sub: She thinks he's loud and incapable. But she was upset with the whole class. She may have identified him as her problem. He was restless. He reads more now.

  p: Yes.

  q: Mainly the matter of concern was that he didn't study, didn't get good grades. I explained his limitations to her and made an estimate of what she could expect him to do. I probably got out the test grades and showed them to her. Her response was that he has to get down to business and get ready for college. [The counselor said in an aside that the boy's father died as a result of the war.] She [the mother] said that the boy didn't seem to be *really* interested in working. She compares him with the older child who is more serious. I couldn't prove this, but I don't think it's real sibling rivalry. She says, "I know he can do better."

Int: What did you do?

Sub: I persisted in telling her that the boy has limitations. I showed her his scores—I worked it in as gently as possible, but explained to her that it was hard on the boy to set standards too high. I pointed out that he is a skills student, that it is unfair to the child to be burdened with such high standards.

Int: You haven't moved her?

Sub: No.

r: [Rephrased as follows: Is this case still open?] Yes.

Int: Can you tell me about a case that's closed?

Sub: A girl whose father died—I carried this girl through this period. Her mother came in to have the girl's course revised. She wanted her to take a business course so she would be prepared to take a job. The girl was upset—she was an only child—and she was concerned about her mother. She was trying to be realistic, and she was willing to change her course. It wasn't a drastic change. She could take typing and shorthand in an academic course. We talked about dating—she was going out with this boy who she thought she could reform. She was having trouble with her mother about it. All during the fall, she came in sometimes once a day, and she talked about death and religion. I notified her teachers. They understood and were easy on the work. When she was going through the death of her father she was concerned mainly about her mother. Her teachers began to be worried—through two marking periods her grades were poor. She had to get more realistic. After the Christmas holidays, she says that things are better—she has an open appointment now.

Int: How do you go about closing a case?

Sub: I don't really ever close a case. She came in frequently at first, then for weekly appointments when I'm behind on my work.

CASE 5:

m: Yes, every time he was late or in the throes of an emotional feeling.

n: Various teachers. The division principal, the counselor, the gamut— you know. The police on one or two occasions, for traffic violations.

o: Mostly about helping him to do better in classes. Some were interested in helping him as a person. Most people are inclined to be **overindulgent**, like giving an exam later when he'd missed it.

Int: Why?

Sub: Because he's a hapless-looking guy.

p: Yes.

q: I interpreted to them some of the ways that ———— [the boy] operated that gave him difficulty in school, that this boy needed to evoke [sic] her. Also, I suggested that in dealing with the teachers that they understand that he should get a grade that he deserves.

Int: What else did you talk about?

Sub: This is a long term thing that's still going on. I also suggested some psychiatric help and they didn't follow up. They said they didn't have the money. Their house eats it all up and what they do. They might not believe in psychiatry, that it is all controlled by destiny.

r: This morning I spoke to his algebra teacher, that ———— [the boy] was behind. That he was going to have to fail him.

The problem of the student discussed by the teacher-counselor in Case 1 appears to have been handled by transferring the student out of the school. The Case 1 material on these questions, therefore, does not provide a description of the procedures of gathering and interpreting information in more routine cases. Although the student discussed by Case 2 may also represent an atypical problem—i.e., the possession of pornographic literature—in both the outside cases there is little active information-seeking activity reported by the interviewees (e.g., neither of them talked to the students' parents) and a singular absence of comments concerning the underlying significance of the students' problems. Considering the responses to previous questions by the cases from the Lakeshore High sample, it is likely that problems similar to those discussed in Cases 1 and 2 would be the occasion for intensive information gathering and extensive interpretation by the counseling personnel.

Case 3 presents an example of differential definitions of student problems from the perspectives of several observers. To the principal's secretary the boy in question was "short, gruff" (which this counselor-teacher interpreted to be "the same experience" as his own), and the father's conception was that of a son "always in trouble" with a "negative attitude." The teacher-counselor, however, suspects that the problem is a "deep-rooted thing," although he reports he found "no behavioral things," that the boy's folder contained "no discipline slips," that the boy's classroom behavior by observation was "peaceful and quiet," and his "personality evaluation is above average."

Differential definitions are also illustrated by Case 4. There is a discrepancy between the teacher's definition of the problem ("loud and incapable"), the parent's feeling that the student is simply not working hard on his studies, and the counselor's imputation of a deeper problem. The counselor's attempt to convince the parent of the student's "limitations" illustrates how the student is redefined by invoking criteria (test grades) not considered relevant by the parent. The parent's interest in sending the student to college received direct confrontation by the counselor, which suggests how student and parental aspirations are articulated with the organizational doctrines and practices of the school. The same counselor's discussion of the student whose mother decided that she must give up college plans shows how counseling can support and implement as well as divert students from their declared educational goals.

It is interesting to note how this counselor arranged for other school personnel to accommodate the student's "crisis." The counselor states that teachers, the principal, and others "understand" the student's problems after she talks to them. The teacher "doesn't report him so much now," or they are "easy on the work," and the principal "has let up on the disciplinary action." Such statements suggest one form of sponsorship that may develop in a system with a highly coordinated counseling program.

In the most recent case reported by the social worker (Case 5), the interpretation of problems as surface manifestations of a deeper underlying psychodynamic problem is most clearly evident. His strong clinical orientation leads, as might be expected, to a recommendation to the parents that their child be given psychiatric treatment.

To summarize this section, we note that our materials suggest that the first mention of a problem leads the counselor and social worker to search for additional information about the student in question. Comments and records about the student's progress through the school system are consulted when his present conduct or problem is being reviewed. When other personnel or parents are approached, considerable information, unofficial as well as official, may appear to alert the counselor or social worker to other difficulties. If the student is "typed" early in the record-keeping process—say in the junior high school—he may be labeled as a student who is "always having problems," a "conduct problem," "emotionally disturbed," and the like.

An interesting feature of the more professionalized counseling personnel's evaluations is that, while their vocabulary has a clinical orientation and substance, the conceptions they use are not necessarily precise. There is not a clear-cut correspondence between the specific terms used to characterize the student and the meanings and referents of such terms. Irrespective of the professional orientation and/or training of the counseling personnel, however, the procedures they reported for handling students are fairly consistent: students are periodically interviewed and encouraged to discuss their "problems." Given this procedure, differences in the professional orientation and training of the counseling personnel are critical for identifying problems in the course of the interviews and for interpreting information to document them.

Another interesting feature of the differential definition of the "problem" is that the definition that is applied to it depends upon how far along the organizational path (i.e., from teacher to administrator to counselor to social worker) the problem is referred. If it does not go beyond the teacher, it may never amount to much; if it reaches the counselor or social worker, then the problem may be defined as "serious." Furthermore, the remedial actions recommended by teachers, administrators, and the less professionalized teacher-counselors tend to be more directly addressed to the manifest problem. They may recommend transferring a student from a class where he is having "run-ins" with the teacher, placing him in a less difficult academic setting, expelling him from school, or some similar action. The recommendations of clinically oriented personnel concerning a similar manifest problem are likely to involve a re-evaluation of the student's biography in the light of whatever new information is obtained, "explaining" the student to his teachers, parents, peers, and others, and arranging for something like a series of therapy sessions designed to explore the problem more extensively to "explain" the student to himself. Thus, the professional orientation of counseling tends to lead to a "managed student" in all areas of his life, including his personal adjustment in school, at home, and with his peers, and his future educational aspirations and life plans.

Professionalization and the record-keeping process. The final set of questions we wish to discuss concerns the kinds of records that are kept about students and the significance of "confidentiality." The nature of the counseling interview (e.g., whether it follows a formalized pattern leading to official records and whether those records are treated as confidential or open to other personnel) is important for assessing the extent to which a counseling system is professionalized. This aspect of professionalization is particularly relevant to the question of how the official or unofficial biography of a student affects his school career and later occupational opportunities when such records are consulted for purposes of making recommendations or providing character references. In the context of our discussion of professionalization of counseling, we expect teacher-counselors to show the least concern about records or about obtaining information that might be viewed as confidential, and social workers to be the most concerned with controlling such information. We asked the following questions:

  s: How do you keep track of the information that you get when you're handling a case? (Asked of Lakeshore High sample.)
  t: Was any of the information about this case recorded anywhere? (Asked of outside sample.)
  u: Who has access to the information while the case is open or closed? (Asked of outside sample.)
  v: Are there any formal records made of the information? What kind of thing do you record? (Asked of Lakeshore High sample.)
  w: How are these records filed? (Asked of Lakeshore High sample.)
  x: Are these files shared among the counselors? Can you give me an example of how this works? (Asked of Lakeshore High sample.)
  y: Do any of the other school personnel have occasion to refer to the files while the case is active or after it is closed? (Asked of Lakeshore High sample.)

CASE 1:
  t: Yes, we have a record for our use—an interview form.
    Int: What was recorded?

Sub: I recorded the basic interview I had and the interview we had with the prosecuting attorney and with the principal. It was recorded in the school files as well as the prosecuting attorney's files.

Int: What happened at the interview with the prosecuting attorney?

Sub: What do you mean what happened?

Int: What did he say?

Sub: It was an interrogation. He was trying to find out what happened. It was a brief sort of thing. He was advised as to what the consequences could be.

Int: What was he advised?

Sub: Legal advice as to what his rights would be.

Int: Who gave the advice?

Sub: The prosecuting attorney advised him.

Int: Who was present?

Sub: The principal, I was, the prosecuting attorney, the boy and the other counselor.

Int: What did the boy say?

Sub: He explained his version of the incident. He claimed he had nothing to do with it. He had not been with the girl. He had been, but not at this time. He denied the accusation.

Int: What happened then?

Sub: The boy was allowed to go back to class. The girl was given a physical examination.

Int: Was the girl a student in your school?

Sub: Yes, an eighth-grade girl.

u: Just the counselors.

Int: Do other people on the staff have access to the files?

Sub: No, not this kind of information.

CASE 2:

t: Yes, in the counselor's file; there are two kinds: the general counselor's file, which is confidential, and the other is the psychiatric and psychological maladjustment, which is secret.

Int: What was recorded?

Sub: The information about the tests and the pornographic material.

Int: Where was it recorded?

Sub: The information about the tests was recorded in the counselor's file and the other in the secret file.

u: The counselors control access to the information—whether the teachers see it or not. Integrity among teachers is not high; therefore it is not wise to give access to all the information.

Int: What do you mean?

Sub: The teacher will indiscriminately refer information to the students and hurt them.

> *Int:* Who has access to the secret file?
> *Sub:* The counselors only.

Both cases quoted above (as well as other interviews in the outside sample) indicate that the counseling personnel share information about students, but that teachers are likely to be barred from materials which are considered confidential, particularly the "serious" information kept in the secret file. Our materials suggest that interviewees in the outside sample were concerned about maintaining a code of ethics or being careful or confidential in their handling of records containing intimate information about students. Some of them (and some teacher-counselors at Lakeshore High as well) noted that they usually destroy material considered intimate after the student graduates from school. It would appear that the notion of confidential information, if not the principle of exclusively privileged material, is a basic aspect of counseling activity and one that concerns even the least professionalized of counseling personnel. The expressed interest in maintaining confidentiality, however, is not carefully articulated, nor is it evident that there are rules for deciding what is to be included in a file, destroyed, or not recorded. The most we can say about the outside sample is that their responses to our questions indicate that matters of confidentiality arise and appear to be concerned with test scores and psychological materials. Mention of more "serious" information was infrequent, and when mentioned the statements were characteristically vague. This may reflect their avoidance or lack of interest in intensively pursuing routine problems.

The cases from the Lakeshore High sample responded to these questions as follows:

CASE 3:

> *t:* I have a notebook. I have all the counselees in here. Some of the pages are blank. Nothing significant. A kid comes in and everything is going well, then there's nothing to note. I started out being very specific, but then I thought, who knows, someone might come along and see the notes. It's confidential. I use this [the book] to write yearly summaries of students. For those who I don't have any notes— I know about these kids [in the book]. A rare instance that you have a great kid.

Int: You make an end of the year report?

Sub: We have to write a summary for each counselee. We have a rating scale for personality, good citizenship, and that sort of thing. It goes to the office.

Int: How do you make a decision to write or not write a note?

Sub: Anything that indicates that the kid is not happy, or makes the kid unhappy, concerned, hostile, or something. For example, the small boy that came in—very good personality. He says "I can't study at home, the TV's on all the time. How can a guy study?"

v: Yes, except for whatever I write to the social worker, if referral is made, but this is on file with the social worker. If we don't have the kids, then in four years we'd have four summaries and recommendations would be made on that basis.

Int: Are referrals to social workers noted in the files?

Sub: Yes, and the principal would note it, too.

w: They're in the cabinet—alphabetized. The test results, the whole history of the kid. You can get a good idea of what kind of kid he is—there are discipline slips, year summaries, the eighth grade reports. We used to have counselor's comments on the end of the counselor's folder. Two years ago, we had a conference and decided they should be limited to counselor's notes, and access limited to teachers, parents, and counselors.

x: Yes, there wouldn't be much need for it though. More with teachers. The teachers would be concerned with our files. The teacher might go to the files to find out why the kid was behaving in a certain way. If something has happened, I would send a note to the division file. One Institute Day, we tried to clarify issues between counselors and teachers. We spent half of the day on this problem.

y: [Rephrased as follows: You mentioned that teachers have access to files.] Yes, I say teachers broadly—all personnel would have access to them. So we have to be cautious what to say. Instead of "Johnny's mother threatened, etc.," "Extreme home conditions. See me."

Int: Does that mean you now have two books?

Sub: Well, really, the book down there is for the school, and my book is for those who want to know more.

Int: If a teacher comes to you and asks about a note, what would you do?

Sub: If I thought that the conditions were affecting his work, etc., I might tell the teacher that there was something at home so important that it is depriving this boy of studies—can't we arrange for some kind of study time or place?

Int: Are teachers satisfied with this?

Sub: Most are satisfied. But if they push me, I might tell them.

[This counselor-teacher was very vague as to the rules at this point.] Some may go to files and say "What is this guy doing for this kid?" They look at the lack of information and think that we're not doing anything.

CASE 4:

   t: Anecdotal information, I take rough notes, when anything unusual occurs. At the end of the week I may merge the conferences. And at the end of the year, I write something on everybody. At the end of the freshman year, I write a long report on every student. "Apparently good adjustment—work up to standard." I'll probably use a check list—something more precise. There's no record system—it's different in different divisions.

   Int: At the end of the year, do you have a tabulation of the number of students you have seen?

   Sub: I report the approximate number of interviews, parents seen, groups worked with.

   Int: Do you have a classification of cases?

   Sub: I see every student three times—getting acquainted, planning programs. Next year we plan to have the students for four years. We'll have a continuing relationship. [The counselor said something about finding out what types of problems students have. She plans to work up a measure of how students feel about the counseling service, what kinds of things they'd like to talk about, any problems they want to talk about immediately.]

   Int: What kinds of problems are listed in your report?

   Sub: Personal, academic, parent relationship, behavior, vocational.

   v: No. Although the files are permanent, all anecdotal material is kept out. We must discuss this problem for a schoolwide policy.

   Int: What do you mean?

   Sub: Some divisions clean out records, others keep them. It should not be a division decision.

   w: They are kept in the division office. I keep duplicates so that it is not seen in too many places. I always get the anecdotal material to the division office as soon as possible for the principal in case he has to handle a case.

   x: Yes. They are in the division office and they can be checked out. If counselors are changed they might want to look at the file. As the system is set up now, we're not supposed to change counselees. A counselor can come to me and ask, "What did you mean by this?" Teachers can refer to the files—this is controversial, but I think this must be [i.e., that the teachers have access to the files]. The social worker's files are not open, but we can get verbal information.

Int: How do you feel about that?

Sub: We'd like a closer relationship. More uniformity in records.

y: Yes. This hasn't concerned the administration as much as it should. We have kept records rather indiscriminately.

Int: Do other personnel have occasion to refer to the files?

Sub: Yes. Teachers. If they are concerned with an individual beyond his grades, they can get test scores through the division.

Int: Do they check out the file with anyone?

Sub: The files are controlled by the division secretary. Counselors can take out folders, but not teachers.

Int: Why would they want to see the files?

Sub: To see a student's grades and progress, to see if there are any problems involved. Also coaches are encouraged to use the material in selecting teams—to find out individual things which are important when working individually with students.

CASE 5:

t: I have a locked file here. What I get this information for is a dynamic picture of what's going on.

v: Yes.

Int: What kind of thing do you record?

Sub: I've been doing summaries which includes family history, developmental history, diagnostic, reasons for referral. It's pretty much like the outline you've been following.

w: I keep them here, but upon closing a case it goes to Miss ——— [Special Services] office and it's there during the summer months when I'm not here.

x: Yes. They're shared among the visiting counselors [i.e., social workers] they are not available to the other counselors.

Int: Can you give me an example of how this works?

Sub: For example, it would be a case where one counselor was handling a kid from another division. [The social worker suggested this might occur where counselors might be handling students from the same family.]

y: No. Not even Mr. ——— [the principal].

Int: What would you do if he asked to see them?

Sub: I'd show it to him. I'd trust him. He's discreet.

Int: Do other personnel have occasion to refer to the file?

Sub: No.

The problem of confidentiality as expressed by the Lakeshore High cases is not only that of controlling access to materials obtained by counseling personnel but also of insuring the proper interpretation of the recorded materials by those personnel who might have access, whether authorized or not, to the files. The problem of interpretation arises as a consequence of the purposefully cryptic entries that the counseling personnel record in the more widely accessible files. Thus, the counseling personnel's lack of authority to control their information leads them to keep two sets of records, a sort of double-entry record-keeping system which produces an official and an unofficial biography of the student. This situation poses a dilemma for the counseling personnel, particularly those whose counseling methods direct them to probe for the "underlying problems." On the one hand they must withhold information from the official files and phrase their entries in a way that will maintain confidentiality. On the other hand, these personnel are concerned that the official files do not give a "true picture" of students and are open to misinterpretation that may harm the students in question. The "see me" notes that are attached to their cryptic entries do not resolve the dilemma, for they present the problem of confidentiality anew when inquiries are in fact made to the counseling personnel for explanations. It may be suggested, however, that insofar as the decision to release or withhold information in such circumstances rests with the counseling personnel, the double-entry record-keeping system does provide them with a measure of information control.

In contrast, the social workers maintain official files controlled by bureaucratic rules that close them to all except other social workers. The assurance that their files are protected by such rules enables them to keep detailed notes of the most intimate information. Although the device of the unofficial file used by the less professionalized counseling staff is analogous to the social workers' privileged file, some concern was expressed that the unofficial file may nevertheless be accessible to non-counseling personnel. The organizational protection of confidential material that is enjoyed by the social workers is another mark of their superior professional status. They are recognized as *the* professional group within the counseling system, and they are the only members privileged to see all information obtained by school personnel concerning students. The bureaucratic rules that control the social worker's file, however, have a corollary in the survival of those files as permanent records of the students' careers within the high school. The disposition of the unofficial files when the student or counseling staff member leaves the system is much more problematic. The social worker's records must be transferred to the central files of the Special Services Division, which is administratively independent of any particular school within the district. The individual counselor, however, may decide that certain information which he has unofficially recorded or carried "in his head" is too confidential to be entrusted to someone who doesn't have the complete picture, and thus may omit, delete, or destroy any reference to it in whatever record remains. The differential organizational control of the disposition of files by social workers and by other counseling personnel may have important consequences for the students' subsequent educational, occupational, and more general life chances. There are occasions when even the closely guarded files of the school system may be opened or "interpreted" to outside agencies when the administrative authorities at the high school or the Special Services Division consider it to be warranted. For example, a prospective employer or the Federal Bureau of Investigation may inquire about a student and request information. In such circumstances, the interpretations made of the materials in the permanent files may be extremely problematic. Of all the personnel interviewed, the social workers were particularly sensitive about the harm that might befall a student as a result of the information they gathered and recorded about him.

Summarizing the responses of our interviewees to these questions, it appears that there is considerable concern among counseling personnel about the confidentiality of their information, and this concern is expressed irrespective of their professional orientation. Our materials suggest that if counselors were given the same authority and administrative support in the control of confidential information as is given to social workers, their professional orientation would probably be more routinely and effectively implemented. As between the teacher-counselor and the counselor, however, the major difference in professional orientation is that the former is less likely to define problems as "serious" and hence not as likely to seek or encounter intimate information from or about the student.

Conclusions. In our discussion of the materials obtained from interviews with counseling personnel we have stressed two major themes: (1) that the implementation of student and parental aspirations is made problematic by the organization of counseling activities within the school system; and (2) that the problematic character of such aspirations must be viewed in the context of the bureaucratization of the counseling system and the emphasis upon the professionalization of its activities. Our materials suggest that the counseling personnel are continually faced with the problem of advising parents to acknowledge "realistically" the "facts" about their children's abilities and aspirations. Our interviewees often mentioned that parents insistently "push" their children into courses and programs which the latter cannot manage, and that they refuse to abandon plans to send their children to particular colleges and universities to pursue careers that the counseling personnel view as unrealistic and unattainable.

These parental efforts are not without effect. Interviews that we obtained with the college placement counselor to supplement those reported above revealed that as students approach their senior year, parents become very active in seeking appointments for conferences with her. In these conferences, this counselor reports that parents insist that she advise and support their children to seek admission to a "good" if not a particular college. The counselor may reveal for the first time the discrepancies between the parents' conceptions of their children's ability and prospects and those of the counseling staff, and she may urge them to reevaluate and revise their plans accordingly. On the basis of such revised plans, the college placement counselor (with the assistance of the student's counselor) may make special efforts to secure admission for the student to *some,* if not the preferred, college. Such assistance may be given in accommodation of parental insistence even to those students who previously had been advised by their counselors not to plan on going to college.

It should be noted here that at Lakeshore High and other schools that serve a strongly college-oriented population there is considerable organizational control over the applications of seniors to colleges. Although seniors are allowed to make appointments to confer with any of the more than 125 college representatives who visit Lakeshore High for recruitment purposes, these representatives are also briefed about students by the counseling personnel. College applications are also controlled by strong suggestions that the student apply to three schools recommended by the counselor and by the kind of letters of recommendation sent to college admissions offices. Thus the distribution of college applications and their outcomes are significantly affected by the judgments and actions of the counseling personnel.

The insistent efforts of parents to realize the educational plans they have made for their children, however, may also produce results that they may not have anticipated or about which they are totally unaware, for their very efforts may lead their children to be identified as a "problem" within the organization. The student's records may become the object of intensive review by the counseling personnel in the course of which not only the student but the parents themselves may be subjected to interpretation and analysis. We have already discussed some of the imputations that may result from such intensive counseling activity and the kinds of records it may leave in its wake. It is this convergence and coordination of the dual organizational concerns—the differentiation and development of talent and the extension of counseling services to facilitate individual adjustment—that has been the focus of our discussion in this chapter.

We suggest that the importance of the counseling system for identifying talent and sponsoring it through high school and into college will grow in significance in those high schools in which a professional counseling orientation is encouraged and enforced from within the school system or imposed from without by state requirements. With such a development our "atypical" case of Lakeshore High School will become a familiar form of high school organization.

5. HIGH SCHOOL BUREAUCRACY

AND SOCIAL MOBILITY

In the preceding chapters we have reported the findings from our study of how one "advanced" high school differentiates students and counsels them toward various educational goals. We have investigated the parents' statements concerning their aspirations and plans to send their children to college, the expression by the students themselves of those aspirations and plans, and their implementation or lack of it by the high school. We have attempted to balance the social psychological emphasis of the studies cited in Chapter 1 that stress the motivations and aspirations of students and parents, the influence of peer and reference groups on student aspiration and performance, and similar variables by presenting an organizational analysis of how student and parental orientations are defined, re-defined, and processed by the everyday activities of a high school bureaucracy that assimilates advanced educational doctrines and practices. The generalizability of our findings are limited by the atypical organizational development of Lakeshore High School. Insofar as such a high school represents a model of future high schools, however, our materials indicate a trend toward the rationalization and bureaucratization of the educational system and, by implication, of the processes of social mobility.

In this final chapter we wish to venture beyond the limitations of our study to consider the consequences of the trend toward the rationalization and bureaucratization of the educational system for the maintenance of an open class system. Our interest in social mobility is related to our conception of the social organization of the high school as a mechanism whereby the student population is differentiated and distributed among the two major lines of future occupational career development, i.e., those occupations which require college training and those which do not. We have used our materials to question the oversimplified formulation of the ascription hypothesis and to stress the importance of the organizational contexts in which students are evaluated as to their ability and potential, informed of their aptitudes, assigned to courses, and thus channeled by the guidance staff into lines of career development. These daily transactions between school personnel and students may be viewed as the practiced and enforced system which largely determines the present and future educational opportunities of students.

How do the increasing emphasis upon testing and counseling and the bureaucratization of such activities in the school system affect the maintenance of education as the major channel of mobility in American society? Or, to phrase the question in the terms of Ralph H. Turner's recent comparative analysis of the American and British educational systems, to what extent is the American system properly characterized as one which organizes and supports "contest" as opposed to "sponsored" mobility?

INDIVIDUAL EFFORT AND ORGANIZATIONAL SPONSORSHIP

Our study provides illustrative data that are relevant for an examination of Turner's analysis of the two educational systems. His analysis proceeds on the assumption that

> . . . within a formally open class system that provides for mass education the organizing folk norm which defines the accepted mode of upward mobility is a crucial factor in shaping the school system, and may be even more crucial than the extent of upward mobility.[1]

He proposes that the organizing folk norm in the United States differs from that in England and as a consequence the relation of

[1] Ralph H. Turner, "Sponsored and Contest Mobility and the School System," *Amer. Sociological Rev.*, 25 (December 1960), p. 856.

the two systems of education to the processes of social mobility are characteristically different. The American and British educational systems are characterized in the following ideal typical terms:

> *Contest* mobility is a system in which elite status is the prize in an open contest and is taken by the aspirants' own efforts. While the "contest" is governed by some rules of fair play, the contestants have wide latitude in the strategies they may employ. Since the "prize" of successful upward mobility is not in the hands of an established elite to give out the latter can not determine who shall attain it and who shall not. Under *sponsored* mobility elite recruits are chosen by the established elite or their agents, and elite status is *given* on the basis of some criterion of supposed merit and cannot be *taken* by any amount of effort or strategy. Upward mobility is like entry into a private club where each candidate must be "sponsored" by one or more of the members. Ultimately the members grant or deny upward mobility on the basis of whether they judge the candidate to have those qualities they wish to see in fellow members.[2]

Turner's characterization of the American educational system as one that promotes a contest among individuals who "have wide latitude in the strategies they may employ" to facilitate their mobility must be modified if our illustrative materials are indicative of a trend in American high schools. Our materials indicate first of all that in the bureaucratically organized high school the day-to-day activities of the school personnel effectively control the access of students to the limited number of curriculums available, particularly their access to the curriculum most instrumental for upward mobility, i.e., the college preparatory curriculum. Our case study suggests that through their control over the student's course programs, the school personnel may include or exclude students from the "contest" and that the "aspirants' own efforts" are neither the only nor the critical determinant of their qualification as "contestants."

This is not to say that the aspirants' efforts are irrelevant to qualifying them for the "contest" or advancing their position within it, but rather that their efforts are not necessarily evaluated, as might be assumed, by academic standards alone. If the SCAT

2 *Ibid.*, p. 856.

scores and grade-point averages of students may be considered indicative of their efforts, our materials suggest that, in a number of cases, students who show such effort may be handicapped or even excluded from the "contest."

It should be noted that the educational system in the United States does manifest all the formal characteristics that Turner attributes to contest mobility. There is an emphasis upon periodic examinations; formalized criteria govern the progress of students in the hierarchy of grade levels; college entrance requirements are not automatically achieved by virtue of enrollment in high school; and college admission is an outcome of a competitive process. Our research, however, supports the view that the student's progress in this sequence of transitions is contingent upon the interpretations, judgments, and action of school personnel vis-à-vis the student's biography, social and personal "adjustment," appearance and demeanor, social class, and "social type," as well as his demonstrated ability and performance. In this respect, mobility in the highly bureaucratized high school bears a striking resemblance to the sponsorship found in graduate departments of universities, in which judgments about the student's maturity, emotional stability, character, and personal appearance are often important determinants of his social mobility.

Secondly, although Turner assumes that the folk norm of contest mobility is "present at least implicitly in people's thinking, guiding their judgments of what is appropriate in many specific matters,"[3] the degree to which such thinking is articulated in the organizational judgments and actions of the school personnel must be viewed as problematic. This is particularly true in an educational system in which school policies are increasingly professionalized and bureaucratically implemented. The advances and setbacks in the process of mobility in such a system are governed less by the folk norms of the larger society than by the doctrines and practices of a professionalized bureaucracy. Insofar as the rationalization and bureaucratization of procedures imply greater "objectivity" in the evaluation of performance and distribution of rewards, it

3 *Ibid.*, p. 856.

might be argued that the application of such organizational techniques represents an institutionalization of the folk norm of contest mobility. Our materials do not support such an argument. Examination of how students are assigned to college and non-college curriculums, distributed among different ability-grouped courses, and identified as various "problems" suggests that the professed ideal of equal access to educational opportunities for those of equal ability is not necessarily served by such procedures.

Indeed, our materials on the differential interpretation of test scores and grade-point averages by school personnel, the definitions and treatment of student "problems," and the organizational activities directed toward facilitating the processing of low performance students toward college entrance indicate that the patterned deviations from bureaucratic procedures amounts to a form of sponsorship. The differentiation of students by objective criteria obviously is not *the* rational basis for the allocation of educational opportunities, for the bureaucracy permits considerable discretion in decision-making. The views of professional educators concerning "adjustment," "motivation," "realistic goals," "overachievers," "participation," and the like are accommodated in the bureaucratic setting, and they constitute significant qualifications of the folk norm of contest mobility. The accommodation of such conceptions has created a complicated system of organizational sponsorship in which discrepancies of ability and performance, aspirations, and realistic possibilities are adjusted, modified, or created in some instances, ignored in others. Decisions for such actions are made by professionals who are guided not by folk norms but by explicit and implicit educational doctrines and practices.

The organizational sponsorship that occurs in American schools may not be as obvious or as explicitly acknowledged as the form of sponsorship that Turner attributes to the British schools. It is quite clear that even in Hollingshead's class-conscious Elmtown the differential treatment and sponsorship of students by school personnel were covertly practiced. Although the bureaucratic organization of the modern comprehensive high school is undoubtedly less vulnerable to the inequities of the social-class pressures documented by Hollingshead, the distribution of educational opportunities is conditioned by decisions and actions that effectively accommodate social-class as well as other information about students.

The rationalization of the school system through the incorporation of the concepts and methods of psychiatry, psychology, and the social sciences has legitimized the relevance of personal and social factors for the interpretation of the "objective" measures of the student's ability and performance. Such factors are explicitly acknowledged as educationally relevant and incorporated into a complex system of organizational policies and procedures. Thus, although testing procedures are extensively employed and course grades are routinely reviewed, the information they provide are in some instances the sole basis for organizational decisions, but in other instances their significance is qualified by considerations of personal and social factors. In such a system, a student's mobility may be more than incidentally contingent upon the sponsorship of organizational personnel who certify him to be a "serious, personable, well-rounded student with leadership potential."

In presenting these objections to Turner's thesis we stress once again the importance of investigating the processes of social mobility at the level of the day-to-day organizational activities in which often unstated rules of mobility are defined and the direction and rate of progress through the system are controlled. Insofar as contest and sponsored mobility are characterizations of organizations, investigation should be directed to the organizationally defined activities of school personnel as well as to the characteristics of individuals who are upwardly or downwardly mobile. One of the critical problems we face in theorizing about comparative differences in the organization and control of social mobility is that the studies utilizing the techniques of large scale survey research are not articulated with the more focused organizational analyses. Generalizing from the findings of either the survey studies, which do not provide data concerning the organizational processes of mobility, or of the limited organizational studies, which cannot claim to be representative or to produce data on a large enough sample, is hazardous.

THE BUREAUCRATIZATION OF SOCIAL MOBILITY

The bureaucratization of the high school is not, of course, a peculiar consequence of the search for academic talent in the "cold war" but a manifestation of the general trend toward the rationalization of daily activities in all spheres of contemporary life. With the progressive differentiation and specialization of functions in modern society, we expect an intensification of attempts to maximize the efficiency of identifying and developing the talent within the population. The identification and development of talent is without question a legitimate concern of the high school, and there are indications that this concern is beginning to stimulate the organization of talent programs at the junior high and elementary school levels. Indeed, many educators have suggested (and the Cleveland, Ohio school system, for example, has long practiced) that students be tested and programmed into several curriculums in the elementary schools.

The scientific status of tests currently in use is ambiguous. It is well known among educators as well as testing psychologists that our present tests are not perfectly constructed. Although test results may be informative with reference to an aggregate population to which tests are administered, they present hazards when applied to individuals. Consequently, their utility as predictive measures of future success is extremely limited. Tests results are nevertheless used as bases for the many organizational decisions that must be made in the processing of large numbers of students by limited and often untrained personnel. The quantitative terms in which test results are expressed provide relatively clear-cut standards by which the most complex and difficult decisions may be bureaucratically routinized.

If the bureaucratization of the school system progressively extends into the elementary school and test scores become the sole basis for identifying the potential ability of students and differentiating their educational experiences, it will become increasingly difficult to determine whether criteria other than test scores are relevant for the identification of academic talent. For if students are tested and differentiated into ability groups and if the differentiation is used as the basis for sectioning them into ability-grouped curriculums, the talent developed by the educational system is automatically limited by the criteria applied to identify it. Thus, an educational system that gears its curriculums to ability groups differentiated early in the educational process is progressively committed to investing its resources (including an intensified guidance service as well as more greatly individualized curriculums) to maximize the "pay-off" of a limited number of "talented" students.

To what degree would such a system maximize the salvage and minimize the wastage of talent in the population? Let us assume that the tests administered to identify talent are valid, i.e., that they do in fact measure intelligence, ability, aptitude, or whatever they are designed to measure. Insofar as any test administered at a given point in time is subject to random if not systematic error, some students included in each of the ability-group categories produced by the tests will be incorrectly classified. A consequence of testing error is that it leads to an unknown proportion of students who are in fact "non-college material" being included among those classified as "college material," while the "non-college material" category will include some who are in fact "college material." Thus, the use of test scores with this built-in error as the basis for assigning students to college and non-college curriculums produces what statisticians call Type 1 and Type 2 errors. The Type 1 error would be the waste of talent that results from the assignment of students who in fact are college material to the non-college curriculum, and the Type 2 error would be the waste of educational resources that results from the assignment of students who are in fact non-college material to the college curriculum. There is no existing method that will eliminate these two types of errors. The best that can be achieved at present is the minimization of one type of error at the cost of maximizing the other, and the decision as to which course of action should be taken is a question of the relative values given to talent and educational resources.

An educational program so singularly committed to the calculation of talent and educational resources would be difficult to implement in the United States. If the folk norm of contest mobility does in fact exert an influence upon the educational system, it is more than likely to resist rather than to support such a rationalization of equal opportunity. A more significant and probably more effective source of resistance to the implementation of such a device is to be found within the educational system itself. Our materials suggest the not unusual use of "non-academic" and other personal and social factors by professional personnel for the classification, evaluation, and counseling of students. The trend toward increasing professional authority concomitant with the rationalization of the educational system significantly limits the development of a completely rational allocation of educational resources. A rational solution to the allocation of educational resources would entail a complete transformation of the professionally oriented policies and practices currently instituted in typical as well as the most advanced school systems.

Our case study suggests the emergence of a different form of the ascription or sponsorship principle of placement implemented by a bureaucratic set of procedures. The characteristics that determine placement by this principle would not be the traditional attributes of caste, kinship, race, sex, or other biologically or culturally determined traits of individuals and groups, but the data of test score records, biographical history of family or personal problems, childhood accidents and traumas, academic difficulties, adjustment problems, and the like. The contingencies of social mobility would be controlled within a bureaucratic setting where professional educational doctrines, policies, and practices are fused with clinical and common-sense conceptions to interpret such information and to differentiate the potentially successful from the failures.

The possibility of systematizing the application of this principle of placement is now at hand. Advances in the theory and technology of computer systems provide techniques of processing large numbers of individuals on the basis of standardized units of information. Such units may contain objective as well as subjective information, facts as well as hearsay, rational as well as common-sense interpretations, thus giving due consideration to education not only as a science but also as an art. Insofar as the gathering, coding, and input of such information are bureaucratically controlled, it would be possible to specify the student's probable access to educational opportunities and future life chances by the processing of his cumulative records. In short, the contingencies of social mobility may be rationalized by the use of computer systems in the form of an actuarial table.

CONCLUSION: SOME EVALUATIVE COMMENTS

In view of the strategic importance of educational organizations for the transmission and implementation of democratic values, the doctrines, policies, and practices of such organizations should be continually examined and subjected to the test of democratic ideals. As sociologists, we have focused attention on the practiced and enforced rules of organizational procedures at Lakeshore High School. As the subject of objective inquiry, the everyday workings of social organizations are not matters to be condemned as immoral, expedient, idealistic, or cynical. Our study was not designed to condemn the modern comprehensive high school as one in which educational standards are confused, criteria of decisions are arbitrary or commonsensical, and sponsorship is based on considerations other than ability and performance. The school system we have studied reveals the patterned deviations from bureaucratic procedures that sociologists have found in other large bureaucracies such as professional, industrial, military, and governmental organizations.

Our interest in the organization and functioning of the school system cannot be described as purely scientific, for field research makes it difficult to separate our roles as social scientists from our roles as private citizens. In the course of the research we both reacted to material which suggested that the bureaucratization of the school system would leave no place for the student to "hide"—specifically, that the day-to-day management of the student's academic, personal, peer, and family problems by school personnel would limit individual variations in self development and social and occupational careers.

It would be presumptuous to issue a set of recommendations concerning the goals of education, the re-organization of existing institutions, and the methods by which those goals might be realized. We propose instead to limit our comments to four organizational features of the school studied that, in our judgment, deserve serious consideration by those concerned with the education of youth.

1. The emphasis upon the recognition and rewarding of ability and achievement is, of course, consistent with the American ideology of equal opportunity for individuals of equal ability. Our study of Lakeshore High School, however, suggests that objective measures of ability may be supplemented by difficult-to-measure attributes. The existence of such cases and the consequences that follow from such misclassifications obviously bring into question the assumption that equal educational opportunities for students of equal capability are insured by the use of testing devices. The use of tests commits the organization to the scores that are produced by those tests as objective bases for decisions and actions vis-à-vis the processing of students. Yet in specific cases, when those results are considered to be inconsistent with other information, the reliability or validity of the test scores may be questioned and taken into account in deciding various courses of action. But if the reliability and validity of the test score in one case are questioned, for whatever reason, the test scores of all cases might also be called into question. The fact that in many cases the test scores are considered to be consistent with other information does not alter the logical implications of attributing less validity or reliability to some test scores than to others.

The problem of insuring equal opportunity, however, is not merely a matter of increasing the reliability and validity of the tests. Rather, the effective realization of equal opportunity is a problem of organizational implementation. However efficient the instruments of identifying capability may be, the distribution of opportunities among students of different levels of ability depends upon whether or not students are in fact organizationally processed with reference to their tested scores.

2. In our discussion of the differential interpretation of test scores and course grades, we barely touched upon the question of the degree to which social class is related to this organizational contingency. In this regard we may ask if Hollingshead's Elmtown study,

which underlined the determinant effect of the student's social-class membership on the way he was handled within the school system, is pertinent to the analysis of the social organization of Lakeshore High, and more generally of large comprehensive high schools in metropolitan areas. We suggest that the organizational accommodation of disputes between parents and counselors highlights the changing relation between the family and school system, and by implication the relation between social-class membership and the organizational processes of the high school. In the current "crisis in education" and the search for talent it has organized, the high school has received increased support from civic and professional groups to create a program that will maximize the development of talent. Such support has tended to increase the autonomy and authority of the school system and to insulate it against the complaints and pressures of middle- and upper-class families.

But the major criterion of the effectiveness of the high school's program for the development of talent is the proportion of its graduates who are admitted to colleges. The proportion of college-*qualified* graduates that a high school produces is limited by the number of students who declare their college-going intentions, whatever their capability. The declaration may be, in the general case, a necessary condition for producing a student who is qualified for college at the end of his high school career. The proportion of graduates who do in fact *register* in colleges is limited by the number of students (again, somewhat independent of their test capability) whose families are able to provide financial support for part or all of their college education (excluding the small number of "complete-expenses" scholarship students). Such conditions would lead high school administrators and their personnel to spend more time with the processing of middle- and upper-class students for college entrance, for it is the students from these social classes who have the best means at hand to validate the effectiveness of the high school's program of developing the talent.

Thus, we suggest that the influence of social class upon the way students are processed in the high school today is reflected in new and more subtle family-school relations than the direct and often blatant manipulation of family class pressure documented by Hollingshead. In one sense, the influences of social class on the treatment accorded students has become a built-in feature of the organizational activities of the modern comprehensive high school, particularly those with highly developed counseling programs. Insofar as the high school is committed to the task of identifying talent and increasing the proportion of college-going students, counselors will tend to devote more of their time and activities to those students who plan and are most likely to go to college and whose parents actively support their plans and make frequent inquiries at the school about their progress—namely, the students from the middle and upper social classes. Thus, as between two students of equal ability who are reported as failing in their courses, if one is a college-going upper-middle-class student and the other a non-college working-class student, how is the counselor likely to handle them? If our assumption is valid, the upper-middle-class student will be called to a conference, inquiries will be made among his teachers, and his parents will be informed of his problems, while the lower-class student, unless he is considered exceptionally bright, may be ignored. The differential attention given students of middle and upper social classes is not here seen as a result of direct class pressures applied by parents, but as an effect of the counselor's conceptions of the type of student who should be doing better, who "won't make it if he doesn't apply himself," whose parents "will be very upset if he isn't accepted at X University," and so on.

3. One of the consequences of the disproportionate attention given to college-going students in the organizational effort to develop talent is that the recognition and exploration, by students as well as school personnel, of the range and variety of talent are limited if not precluded. We do not refer here simply to the frequently discussed problem of the discriminatory effects imposed by academically oriented high schools upon students who do not plan to go to college. We refer to the consequences of the organizational emphasis on talent upon the development of the full range of individuality among the student population, and most particularly among the college-going students. The high school as a "talent farm" that attempts to accommodate parents, colleges, and the demands of the larger society may produce seniors who are college-

qualified but not interested in a broad educational experience. The differentiation of college-going and non-college-going students defines the standards of performance by which they are evaluated by the school personnel and by which students are urged to evaluate themselves. It is the college-going student more than his non-college-going peer who is continually reminded by his teachers, counselor, parents, and peers of the decisive importance of academic achievement to the realization of his ambitions and who becomes progressively committed to this singular standard of self-evaluation. He becomes the future-oriented student interested in a delimited occupational specialty, with little time to give thought to the present or to question the implications of his choice and the meaning of his strivings.

We are not subscribing to the notion that the high school should provide a period of mindless fun and games to distract adolescents from the presumed confusions of their period of personal growth. American adolescents have too long been victims of their own publicity, which describes them as a population given to performing personal rituals with extravagant enthusiasm or hopeless despair. In this respect, the search for talent in the high school has generated an atmosphere in which academic achievement provides a meaningful basis for esteem and prestige within the peer group as well as the school system. We are concerned, however, that the organizational emphasis upon talent and the pursuit of narrow specialties virtually ignores the significance of adolescence as a period during which individuals may explore the alternatives of personal style, interests, and identity. With the diffusion of specialized educational programs from the graduate school through colleges into the lower school systems, the adolescent is forced to make decisions and declare choices from a range of alternatives he can hardly be expected to know.

4. Some may argue that although the contemporary educational system has (perhaps unnecessarily) pushed the college/non-college decision into the freshman year in high school, the college-going alternative is open to all students. What we take to be the serious issue is that the college/non-college decision has become *the* decision with reference to which the student is assigned to courses,

evaluated as to performance, and organizationally processed. It should certainly be no surprise that counselors find in the course of their counseling activities that students are concerned with a variety of personal problems other than whether or not they are achieving up to their ability. Indeed, how can we doubt that they are troubled by feelings of uncertainty, inadequacy, futility, self-pity, and so on when they are continually reminded that their present actions are fraught with consequences for the future?

In a high school geared to the development of talent, however, the student discusses such feelings at his peril, for they are not viewed as simply normal manifestations of adolescence compounded by the stresses generated by the organization itself. It would not be an exaggeration to state that the high school as a "talent farm" produces its own problems, and that it has developed a "clinic" to deal with them. The sense in which the high school has become a "clinic" in the name of developing talent has, in our judgment, ramifications that extend far beyond providing counseling and guidance services to the student population. Suspending the questions of the validity of interpretations of student problems made by the counseling personnel and the modes of treatment that are prescribed and practiced, the issue which must be addressed is whether or not the school is or should be authorized to engage in such activities. We do not doubt that from a psychiatric point of view the behavior of some students may be diagnosed as serious problems that call for specialized treatment, but these students must certainly represent a small fraction of the student population. We do question, however, the propriety of a procedure that routinely assigns students to counselors who not only monitor their progress but actively seek and probe for "problems." This is an invasion of privacy, however disguised it may be by an ideology of service and "help," and an invasion during a period when maintaining the privacy of unique personal experience may be critical for the adolescent's awareness of his own individuality. What is even more disturbing is the prospect that this solicitous treatment will produce a new generation of youth socialized to the practice of easy confessions and receptive to "professional" explanations of who they are and what they aspire to become.

In this volume, we have advanced the view that the modern comprehensive high school is characterized by a highly organized effort, implemented by bureaucratic procedures, to identify and develop the talent distributed among its student population. We do not question the relevance or legitimacy of the high school's current concern and involvement in this effort. Clearly, the search for talent is not simply a manifestation of the "crisis in education" but a consequence of the more general demands imposed upon the educational system by a society increasing in scale and complexity. The American school systems have responded to these demands with actual and suggested re-organization of curriculums, experimentation with new methods of teaching, institution of long-range research programs, and other efforts. In this study we have attempted to explore how organizational accommodations to scale and complexity have transformed the conception and function of the school system, and how the consequences of this transformation might affect the socialization of the student population as individuals and as members of the adult society.

APPENDIX *

Our single case study is intended not to test hypotheses but to explore some general notions about the impact of organizational procedures and professional ideologies on the careers of high school students. Our interview materials serve basically as illustration.

Our theoretical orientation leads us to an interest in the categories by which actors in everyday life organize their thoughts and experiences. We have assumed that the common-sense character of everyday knowledge and its vague and taken-for-granted qualities allow the actors to assume that each "knows" what the other intends even though this is not checked out by either party. Much of the communication is not publicly stated but remains private to the communicants, yet these elements of communication are assumed to be integral features of their interaction. How the researcher comes to conceive, study, and infer such processes as "defining the situation" and "taking the role of the other" is basic to our substantive interests. Questions about how personnel in the educational system conceive of their students and how routine organizational decisions are made require a flexible methodology and must reflect the ways in which persons in everyday life generally conceive of objects and events. Our methodological position can be stated as follows:

1. To formulate standardized questions about the workings of the school, we had to assume that both the respondents and the

* Prepared by Aaron V. Cicourel.

researchers shared similar information about school organization and operations.

2. We decided to use open-ended questions because they permit more flexible questions and answers. We avoided fixed-choice questions because they (a) assume invariant meanings to words and sentence structure; (b) may impose the interviewer's perspective on the subject; and (c) rule out the actor's point of view. We did not feel that the obvious advantages in economy of question-asking and accuracy of coding outweighed the disadvantages of fixed-choice questions.

3. Fixed-choice questions with focused probes would presuppose the very knowledge we were seeking, namely, the thoughts and language used in educational settings by which students, their activities, and their futures come to be evaluated and acted upon by organizational personnel. Fixed-choice questions tend to structure the definition of the situation, i.e., "educate" the subject to the researcher's definition of what is felt to be important. While a pretest might help to narrow more accurately the choices to be presented, the researcher cannot be certain that the choices contained in the questionnaire or interview schedule are congruent with the subject's knowledge.

In sociology we seldom are able to spell out our theoretical and substantive issues clearly, and the questions we use are not always precise translations of theoretical material into operational procedures. Thus, coding operations are often difficult to justify. Our coding amounts to a content analysis of a range of responses that presumably reflects the actor's interpretation of the question asked. This content analysis is difficult to do "objectively" in such a way that anyone could readily arrive at the same results. What we "counted" in our study as an instance of something cannot be viewed as independent events, not really additive, and hence not subject to literal statistical tests of significance. Literal hypothesis-testing using statistical tests of significance assumes that the "counts" in a given cell are "identical." Our coding operations would not justify such an assumption.

We felt that the counselor materials were sufficiently revealing in raw form to illustrate our theoretical interests. Unfortunately, therefore, our mode of inference relies upon a mixture of theoretical propositions and common-sense understandings, rather than carefully deduced rules for assessing the import of the data. We have attempted, wherever possible, to lean upon our theoretical notions to convince the reader that our materials are meaningful, rather than upon an unwarranted measurement scale. This means showing how our theoretical framework makes explicit provision for the kinds of descriptions revealed in the responses obtained. The connection between the descriptions provided by our respondents and the organizational workings suggested by our theory is not always obvious, and we are often forced to assume that the reader's interpretation coincides with our own in order to warrant our inferences.

Another way in which we have presented our materials is through the use of coded responses to open-ended questions with focused and unfocused probes. In the case of our student sample we did not use many of the questions because of difficulties in developing rules for coding the responses. Later in this appendix, we show the reader, by examples, how actual responses were coded; it was felt that this material would give the reader some idea of how the connection between coding category and actual response was achieved. The first five cases that were relevant to the coding procedures employed were used each time. The cases are not always clear-cut examples of precise correspondence with our coding procedures; there are a few ambiguous examples. This is sometimes the result of the ambiguous character of the response or the problems attending the construction of the precise coding rules. These shortcomings in methodological procedures, of course, point to more fundamental difficulties contained in formulating precise theoretical propositions in sociology. We know more about the bureaucratic organization of the school system than we do about how the actor (in this case, the student and the parent) perceives and interprets his environment. Hence, we found that questions asked of counselors were almost always usable, while those directed to students and parents were less so unless the queries involved specific organizational activities associated with school.

Finally, we have also presented as a portion of our materials the factual information recorded by the school personnel: grades;

test results; and evaluations that lead to the assembly of behavioral categories for describing students as "incorrigible," "maladjusted," and the like, and to the assembly of organizational designations, such as "underachiever," "honor student," and so on.

This latter kind of data can be questioned if one asks how such designations as "underachiever" were decided by school personnel. In this case the designations become dependent variables. If the researcher decided to treat them as "outcomes" directly influencing the student's career and his status within the school organization, these labels can be viewed as independent variables. They become independent variables if the school personnel honor such labels as indicative of certain kinds of behavior and ability without questioning the criteria that led to the initial labeling process, *and* if they then proceed to use such designations as criteria for, say, recommending a student for college entrance or denying him certain school privileges. When such categories as "honor" student are treated as dependent variables, then actual grades and test scores become the independent variables and can be viewed as literal, at least in part. The qualification stems from the fact that we know that school personnel do not employ consistent cut-off points or absolute criteria for grades and test scores. Therefore, statistical correlations are not warranted unless we could somehow construct similar measures for the other criteria that are used. These other criteria, such as "having the right attitude," "reading widely," and the like, are not easily measured. We argue for the inclusion of these nonmeasurable contingencies of everyday and official social action in the school, even when so-called objective test materials are used for evaluating students, because the nonmeasurable criteria are integral features of the sense made of the so-called objective data. The fact that test materials themselves are subject to fluctuations makes day-by-day evaluations based upon situational definitions and social stereotypy all the more difficult to measure with conventional measurement systems.

The material in Chapter 4 is derived from interviewing counselors about routine organizational practices. The counselor's conceptions are treated as "literal" and "real," under the assumption that our method of interviewing reveals the basis for his daily routine decisions.

The temporal conditions of gathering the data make it difficult to claim that we obtained a single "snapshot" of the school, because our samples were not interviewed at one particular point in time. Our interviews, therefore, reflect events that occurred before the start of the study as well as those that took place after the study began. We believe that our method of interviewing overcame some of these obstacles, but an implicit assumption remains: the occasions of our interviews presuppose that the material elicited reveals invariant decision-making elements. This assumption is, of course, a difficult one to make. But our theoretical framework actually makes this assumption part of our research interests. The "counting" operations we impose upon our materials presupposes that our "one-shot" interviews would yield the same results when repeated over time. Such operations may structure the problematic character of routine day-by-day organizational procedures in a fortuitous manner. The influence of social imputations, personal qualities, physical appearance, "proper" deferences, and "adequate" motivation, are factors that are difficult to measure precisely, yet they constitute a set of qualitative variables that cannot be ignored.

So-called objective factors, because of their "presentable" character, are used frequently to analyze student progress and ability. It is easier to present "facts and figures." Sociological theory, however, tells us that bureaucratic organization may be characterized as efficient and as a device for avoiding responsibility. The "facts and figures" may simply be devices whereby bureaucratic organization defends decisions that are not susceptible to and available for rational analysis. We have assumed that the critical organizational decisions can be described roughly but are not measurable with our present state of knowledge.

How the interviews were conducted. Our interviews were guided by some explicit theoretical assumptions as well as by many vague ideas about what we were trying to obtain in the way of data. The guiding theoretical assumption we followed was that most subjects in everyday life are not able to articulate very clear-cut answers to most sociological questions even if such questions are couched in the language of everyday life. We reasoned that such questions must necessarily be vague in order to fit the kind of general discourse usual in daily life. Not that specific questions cannot be answered, but we assumed that even though the kinds of questions we asked can be phrased specifically, we doubted they could be answered specifically unless we "educated" (e.g., used fixed-choice questions with) our respondents. This does not mean simply asking leading questions, but asking questions ordinarily asked in survey research. Hence, we asked primarily open-ended questions with probes that in themselves were often vague. Our interest lay in gauging what kinds of knowledge our subjects possessed about various matters. We further assumed that by using probes such as "How's that?" and "Could you tell me more about that?" we would make the interview troublesome for our subjects.

We therefore expected to annoy subjects slightly until we were satisfied that they did not know much about the questions we asked. The annoyance technique became somewhat risky, of course, but we felt it important enough to attempt this line of questioning. Some of the drawbacks in our procedure should be obvious. First, we received, as expected, answers that were difficult to code. One might question the usefulness of obtaining data that is difficult to code. But our theory required that we do this, because the theory is not sufficiently developed so that structured questions with structured responses could be asked without deliberately forcing particular answers and running the risk of falsely supporting or discrediting the theory.

Our typical strategy was to ask the question in a general way that was both factual and assumed to be known or "obvious" to the subject, but in a way that carefully avoided giving the subject any help. The critical problem lay in the extent to which the interviewer would let the respondent "off the hook." We followed the initial question with some noncommittal probe that would not let the subject "off the hook" until we were satisfied the subject did not know the answer, knew it in a vague way, or could answer with some degree of specificity. The vagueness was important. Unlike most categories in social research, which run from poor to excellent, from feeling strongly about something to not caring, and the like, vagueness as a definite property of our data interested us because this is what our theoretical framework leads us to expect.

The problem of recording the circumstances under which each of us thought that the subject was vague, or when other difficulties occurred, leaves much to be desired since we did not tape our interviews, although we did try to take verbatim notes. But even tapes would pose problems of coding because it would be impossible to show in the publication how each interview answer was coded, so that each reader could decide for himself that the coding was consistent with his interpretation of the material. As in any research where the answers are open-ended, the reader must take the coding procedure on faith, for it would occupy the largest part of any book on research if included.

Several of our questions failed to produce sufficient information to warrant discussing them. These questions represent situations where we were trying to obtain more subtle measurements by being as vague as we could about the problem at hand. We apparently succeeded in being so vague that our subjects could not answer very coherently. These failures to secure subtle measurements clearly represent defects in our questions. The only positive thing we can say here is that the questions that failed were not crucial and did not undermine the issues we set out to explore. They represented occasions where we sought independent information for the same theoretical notion for which we already had initial sources of data.

As our general strategy, we asked a series of questions on the same point in order to have a number of questions to explore the same concept. The logic resembled that of a survey. All schedules were standardized, and each of us attempted to indicate how we deviated from the schedule in the course of the interview. This material indicating the deviations has been included in our presentation of the example materials. We have not included in our interview materials other questions that appeared in our schedules, the respondents' answers to them, or the probes that followed, because these presented difficulties of presentation within our space limitations. A question might also be raised here on the manner in which interviewing procedures used differ from depth interviewing techniques. The present procedures differ in that they always begin with standardized questions and often employ unfocused probes. They do not attempt to go much beyond the immediate standardized question suggested by the theoretical framework. The interviewer's probes were not designed to follow the initial question wherever it takes him.

Coding Rules for Questions and Tables Presented in Chapter 2, with Examples*

Table 2.2

QUESTIONS: What do you think your child would like to do after leaving high school? (If the parent did not mention college plans, the following question was asked: Does your child plan to go to college?)

Answers coded as "yes" are now presented by subject code and actual response:

3. I suppose go to college and take the premed curriculum.

4. I don't know . . . [Does your child plan to go to college?]
Yes.

5. He wants to be a mechanic for the past two years . . . [Does your child plan to go to college?]
Yes he does. And he also likes music and he's real good in that.

6. He hasn't said very much at all. He came home and said "I would like to be a doctor." [Does your child plan to go to college?]
Yes.

9. I don't have no idea. [Does your child plan to go to college?]
Yes. On his own he plans to.

Answers coded as "no" (and there were only two) are now presented:

80. He wants to go to mechanical or engineering . . . He likes to work with motors . . . [Does your child plan to go to college?]
He doesn't plan to go . . .

86. [Child is mentally retarded.]
Answers coded as "don't know" are now presented:

1. Well, I don't know, you know, service business, he has that to look to. [Interviewer asked if she had talked to him about it.] He doesn't know if he wants to go to college; he's talked about taking music. [Does your child plan to go to college?]
He doesn't know.

14. All that he says anymore is that he wants a business of his own. Before that he said he was going to join the Navy as soon as he was 17. [Does your child plan to go to college?]
He doesn't say yes or no. I don't know.

15. I wouldn't know what he wants. If he's poor or average in arithmetic he couldn't take engineering. I feel that if you're a boy you should study law. I think he [the husband] wants to push that thing. I think I'll do it too. [Does your child plan to go to college?]
I hope he does.

* The illustrative cases presented were taken from the total sample as they occurred. The first five relevant cases were used for each category.

20. Well, she has been considering nursing, baby nursing. She also likes office work. [Does your child plan to go to college?]

I couldn't say that. I don't think so.

31. She said she wanted to be a nurse. [Does your child plan to go to college?]

I don't know.

Table 2.3

QUESTION: Do you remember the first time that the subject of college was discussed?

Responses coded as "elementary school" are as follows:

3. This was just an assumption. Oh, 6 years old or 7 I guess.

5. Oh, from little children up.

6. I think he has always taken this for granted.

8. Oh, I think it was just accepted. You know that this is just the way it was.

9. Probably when he was in the first grade.

QUESTION: How old was your child then?

3. [Not asked. Response assumed given above.]

5. Fourth or fifth grade, nine years old.

6. Well, two or three years ago he mentioned college for the first time. He was at a football game.

8. About ten years old.

9. Six.

Responses coded as "junior high" were as follows:

12. Over a year ago and was brought up over watching a television program.

25. It seems to me it has always been with us.

34. It's been discussed since her eighth year of school. We discussed college.

45. I think in her last year of junior high we were talking of her going to Lakeshore High and the subjects she would take in college.

46. Two years ago.

QUESTION: How old was your child then?

12. 12½.

25. Seriously, this last year, 14.

34. 13.

45. 13

46. 12.

QUESTION: Has there ever been any question about whether your child would go to college?

Responses coded as "financial" problems were as follows:

5. Money.

11. The only question that would come up would be the financial question. I told my husband "I won't take no for an answer." Even if he has to go into the city.

13. Nothing other than financial.

14. [The interviewer was unable to record a verbatim response but noted that the subject mentioned money as a problem here. Another part of the schedule shows that actual remarks were made about older children with respect to financial difficulties and going to college.]

16. Financial! Scholastically, another problem.

Responses coded as "grades" for "any question about going to college:"

31. [Subject had earlier stated doubts about going to college and specifically mentioned the student's grades.]

52. I don't know whether he'll be able to go to college. They're so crowded and we'll have to see what comes. [The subject did not specifically say that grades would be a problem in this context even when asked directly. However, throughout the interview the student's troubles with grades were the subject of many added comments.]

53. [This is a case where the interview material is not available in verbatim form and the interviewer made inferences from remarks made throughout the interview about the student's difficulties with junior high and high school grades. The parents indicated that college had always been discussed around the house but that the boy was not taking a college preparatory program because of his grades.]

85. Yes, of course there's a question about requirements—about getting into college. Colleges are hard to get in now, and they won't take an average student.

Responses coded as "interest" for "any question about going to college:"

9. Yes, there has. That he will eventually go to college . . . I'm sure he will go. Someday he will make up his mind. He might be 20 or 21 when he does, but that he'll go I'm certain. [Throughout the interview this parent kept referring to the lack of concern with school work. He apparently has the capability but simply avoids telling them about school work or doing it.]

26. Well, yes, finances and well . . . She says that "after my first year of high school I'll know if I want to go on with a college course." That's about all.

32. Yes, he has not been interested since junior high. He didn't care much for school.

88. [This subject's parent was not asked this question because the inter-

viewer felt she had effectively answered it earlier when she stated she hoped her daughter would go to college. She then indicated that the daughter was only interested in finishing high school.]

> Responses coded as "no" to "any question about going to college" and also revealing the "taken for granted" character of some responses [also shown in the responses coded as "elementary school" above]:

3. Oh, no!

4. No.

5. We hoped . . . We planned for it a number of years ago, so I would say it was definite planning.

8. I don't think so. I think he himself has always thought so.

10. No, 'cause I'd work if I had to.

Table 2.6

QUESTION: What sorts of requirements does he have to meet for college entrance?

> The code for this question is given in the text (see p. 50). The examples are as follows:

TYPE I:

13. Two majors and two minors, two years of language, two years of science, two years of math, four years of . . . I think, of English. They are encouraging two years of language.

35. Four years of English; lab science and general science wanted by most colleges; and language, women's colleges require it; two years of math; three of history.

63. It depends on the school, of course. Two years of language, two of science, three of math, four years of English, P. E. I don't know beyond that.

6. I'm guessing; I know he has to have four years of English, two years of math, one or two of science, and language.

60. Oh, yes. [A pause.] The standard A.B. requirements is what he needs. Tom ought to have three years of language if he's interested in science. Don had four years of math, English, general science, biology, and chemistry; the usual courses of civics, history, and Spanish. Tom's course would be the same. I regard four years of mathematics as absolutely necessary.

TYPE II:

4. You know, English, a couple of sciences, I guess, and languages.

8. I imagine he has to have two or three years of science, math, and maybe German.

9. Three to four years of English, three years of math, three of foreign language, which he won't like. He is taking courses that will get him into most universities.

1. [Subject began with:] Well, language I guess . . . and four years of English. [She stopped and said:] Gee, they send all that information from the high school. Wait, I'll get it for you. [She brought the interviewer the form sent by the school.]

10. I don't remember exactly, I know there is four years of English, two years of language. Oh, I guess they'll tell him what he needs at the high school.

TYPE III:

2. I have no idea. That is for my husband.

3. They've been changed so. We had a couple of sessions at Lakeshore High. They did mention it but I don't remember. We'll check when they get started.

Table 2.7

QUESTION: Did you attend the meeting at Lakeshore High School held for parents of entering freshmen last February?

This question required only a simple "yes" or "no" answer. Actual examples are not given since there were no problems of coding encountered.

Table 2.8

QUESTION: Have you talked with anyone about college requirements?

Responses to this question were coded as "no" if the statements were as follows:

1. No, I haven't.
2. Not me, my husband knows them.
3. Not specifically, because we just assume the boys know what to do.
8. No.
13. We just read what the school put out for college preparatory.

Responses were coded as "yes" if the statements were as follows:

4. Only because of my older daughter. They had a conference at the high school. [Which the respondent attended.]
5. Yes.
9. No, other than our friends.
10. No, other than the counselor.
11. No, except the counselor.

Table 2.9

QUESTIONS: Have you had anything to do with planning your child's high school program? In what way?

Responses of subjects 6 through 9 were selected arbitrarily to illustrate the coding of recommended college courses.

6. Yes.

Well, we had to help him decide on a language. Whether to take biology the first year, whether to take straight English and straight social studies, and about his minor, like band or something else.

7. Yes.

She had a long list of electives and this question of high school curriculum came up at the same time as those for the eighth grade. She asked me what to take. I told her to take fine arts in the eighth grade and then she turned out to like it. I don't know what her program is exactly. We had a long talk about taking Latin; I told her to take it in the first year so she could find out if she could do it or not.

8. Yes.

It was a cooperative thing. We talked over the subjects he could take. He was quite definite in his own thinking. We weren't too sure. We wanted the combined course and he wanted to take them separately. He is taking them separately. He wants to take four years of language, science and everything.

9. Really, no.

They sent home a lot of material. He already knew what he wanted to do or to take. There isn't much choice; we do want him to take biology instead of general science. He's already had two years of general science in junior high school.

Table 2.10

QUESTION:

   h: I see that you had to choose between Plan I and Plan II. What plan did you choose?

   i: Does it make any difference what plan you choose?

   j: How do you mean?

Responses coded as "knows difference between Plan I and Plan II" are illustrated in the following:

1. *h:* Plan II was a regular course and Plan I was a college preparatory course.

   i: One of them is a college preparatory course.

   j: You take a foreign language, maybe . . . oh, I don't know. Four years of math, and a science.

4. *h:* I don't know. I hear of them. Maybe I did choose. One is going to college and the other isn't. Isn't that right? [Interviewer: Yes.] Well, I'm going to college.

   i: I think it does in the courses you take. I'm not quite sure.

   j: I don't know. I wish I knew.

8. *h:* I knew I wanted to go to college.

   i: One is to go to college and one wasn't.

   j: One prepares you to go into the world right after high school. The other is to go to college.

13. *h:* Yes. I think I chose Plan I.

   i: I think Plan I was where you took the language and Plan II was take science. I think Plan I says you do go to college and Plan II you don't. They passed out a form explaining this.

   j: I said I did plan to go to college. ["Make any difference?"] I believe it makes a difference in the courses you take or what level of courses you take.

19. *h:* Plan I was college and I'm going to college.

   i: Yes, Plan II you don't have to take a certain amount of solids.

   j: For Plan I you have to take them.

Responses coded as "does not know difference between Plan I and Plan II" are presented in the following:

3. *h:* I don't know. [Told by interviewer.] I chose Plan I.

   i: Yes. I chose Plan I because I want to go to college and get a good occupation.

   j: I always pictured that if you didn't go to college you'd end up a garbage man or something and you'd be unhappy.

6. *h:* One plan was combined studies and the other . . . I really don't know. [Told by interviewer.] Oh, I know. If you want to go to college or not.

   i: They try to get you into the courses to go to college if you want to go. If you just want to get out of school I guess they tell you how to do it.

7. *h:* Combined studies and separate. [Told by interviewer.] Oh, yes. I think I went into the college preparatory.

   i: I think it does in your classes.

   j: If you don't plan to go to college, you don't need a foreign language, I guess.

9. *h:* I chose Plan I.

   i: I'm not sure what that is. I'm not sure what the difference between the plans is. [Told by interviewer.] I chose the college.

    j: [Interviewer asks: What is the difference between the plans?] I'm not sure. As the four years progress you get a chance to meet the people from the colleges and then you get coached on how to get in and the advantages and disadvantages of the different colleges. If you don't go to college you can't get ahead in life.

10. *h:* I'm not sure what you mean. There's a combined study course. [Told by interviewer.] Oh, oh, I see. I chose the college one.

   i: The college plan gave you the courses most useful for getting into college.

   j: The other course wasn't so hard; it was just so you could graduate and get a job.

Table 2.11

QUESTIONS: What sorts of entrance requirements do you have to meet to get into college?

   a: Have you talked to anyone about college requirements?
   b: With whom did you talk?
   c: What did he (she, they) tell you?
    The code for this question is given in the text (see p. 45.) The examples are as follows:
    TYPE I:

4. I think . . . one year lab science. I don't know how many years of math. English. Language, at least two years.

   a: No.

6. Language, two years of math. I don't know how much of science. If you go to engineering college you don't need four years of language. If you want to be an engineer you have to take more science and math, I guess.

   a: No.

8. We learned to graduate from high school we have to have four years of English and one year of math. For college you need: two years of math, three years of language, two years of history to graduate from high school, a lab science, one year, four years of gym.

   a: No, well, yeh.
   b: My parents, my uncle.
   c: They didn't know. My sister is applying for college. I found out that most colleges will accept you if you've taken good courses.

12. I've seen a piece of paper in the office once. It says something like two years of language, four years of algebra or math, four years of English,

three or four of history, eight semesters of gym. You have to take chemistry and things like that.

a: No.

13. They gave us a list. Four years of English, three years of math, two years of language, two—three years of science, four years of gym. You have to join some extracurricular activity. It's required in some colleges and not in others.

a: Yes.

b: Friends.

c: We discussed what colleges we want to go to and what you have to take for how long. I also talked to my parents.

TYPE II:

3. I think . . . two years of any language. I don't know how many years of algebra. Four years of English, I guess cause they tell you to. That's all.

a: I haven't actually talked to anyone about college requirements, but I have talked about going to college.

b: My parents.

7. Language, and for a teacher's college a two or three average. Good high school record. English, algebra, history.

a: To friends.

c: They agreed that language and most of the basic subjects were good. My brothers said get good grades in your basics, like English, algebra, history.

11. Sixteen or sixteen and one-half credits; two years language, two years history, English, four years of science. I can't think of anything else.

a: No.

16. One year algebra, four years of English, two years of science, four years gym, two to three years of history.

a: No.

34. They say a foreign language for three years. Everyone has to have four years of English, science and a lab course. [Interviewer: Anything else?] That's all I know.

a: No.

TYPE III:

5. I'm not too sure. Two years foreign language. That's all I know about it.

a: Well, with my counselor; no, I guess not. She was telling us a little about college but mainly high school.

c: She told us her job is to help out freshmen with any problems and what college they want to go to.

23. [No response. Interviewer: What courses, say?] Sort of depends on the college, doesn't it? [Interviewer: Which do you want to go to?] Well, Smith is hanging up there. [Interviewer: Smith, then.] I'm not sure really. I know they get the junior year abroad. I guess algebra might help me get in.

    a: Not requirements, but only about where we want to go.

    b: My friends and family.

    c: Quite a few of them [friends] didn't like the idea of going to an all girls' school.

30. Depends on the college. [Interviewer: Do you plan to go to college?] Yes. [Interviewer: What kinds of courses are you planning to take?] I don't know. I'm taking four years of science. I guess that helps you get in.

    a: No.

36. I haven't any idea except that you have to have at least three years of a language.

    a: No.

TYPE IV:

2. I don't know. I think you have to take a couple of years of Plan I. I don't know which college I'm going to, so I don't know.

    a: No.

15. I was talking to this lady. It's different for different colleges. [Interviewer: Are there any required courses?] I really don't know. I don't worry about it now. They say after four years here you'll know what you want to take.

    a: This lady.

    b: Miss _____ [Counselor].

    c: She just told us she'd help us about college plans. She said some require high grades and things like that.

32. I wanted to go to Ohio State. So that means the top twenty per cent. [Interviewer: Are there any course requirements?] I don't know.

    a: Just my father.

    b: We have a college entrance book.

    c: We looked at the book and it just said whether it was coed and stuff like that.

35. No.

    a: My sister. She went to junior college.

    c: She said it wasn't as hard as most schools, but hard enough.

45. At Illinois you have to have a three average. At Wisconsin you have to have more than a three average. [Interviewer: Do you have to take any particular courses?] I don't think so. I think if you want to get a scholarship you take some particular courses in your senior year.

    a: No.

Interview Schedules

Let me tell you briefly what this interview is about. Our study is concerned with the future plans of high school students, and how decisions about those plans are made. We are interviewing parents, students, and school officials so as to obtain as much information as possible about how students plan for the future. In our interview with you we are particularly interested in your views about this matter.

Before we begin our interview, do you have any questions?

1. First, we'd like to know a little about your child's work in junior high school. *How did your child do in junior high school?*
   a. (Whatever the response to this question, ask:) *How do you mean?*
   b. (Whatever the response to 1 above ask:) *How were you informed about your child's work in school?* (Explore possible sources, but do not push with leading questions.)
   c. (Depending on the response, ask:) *What other information did you receive about your child's work in school?*
   d. *How often did such news reach you?*
   e. *Have you ever contacted any of the people at school about your child?*
   f. (If yes:) *When was the last time you called?*
   g. *How did you come to call?*
   h. *What happened?*
2. *Has the school ever contacted you about your child's work there?* (Indicate that question does not refer to report cards—rather to other kinds of contact.)
   a. (If "yes":) *Who made the contact?*
   b. *How was the contact made?*
   c. *What was the contact about?*
   d. (If the school requested some action on the part of the parent, then ask:) *What did you do about it?*
3. *How do you think your child's work compares with others in his class?*
   a. (If respondent gives general response, then ask:) *Why do you think that?*
   b. *Do you think your child is doing the best he can?*
   c. *Could you tell me a little more about that?*
4. *What do you think your child would like to do after leaving high school?*
   a. *How do you feel about what he wants to do?*
   b. *Have you talked to your child about his future plans?*
   c. (If "no" then ask:) *Do you plan to talk to your child about his future plans?*

   d. (If "yes" then ask:) *What do you expect to tell him?*

   e. (If "yes" to *b*, then ask:) *When was the last time you talked to him about this?*

   f. *Can you tell me about the talk you had with him?*

5. (If college plans are not discussed in 4 above, then ask:) *Does your child plan to go to college?*

   a. (If "no" then:) *Was the possibility of your child's going to college ever considered?*

   b. (If "no" to *a*, then:) *Could you tell me more about that?*

   c. (If "yes" to *a*, then:) *What happened?*

6. (For those whose children are planning to go to college:) *Do you remember the first time that the subject of college was discussed?*

   a. *How old was your child then?*

   b. *Did you talk with your child about it?*

   c. *When was the last time you talked to your child about his college plans?*

   d. *What did you talk about?*

   e. *Has there ever been any question about whether your child would go to college?* (Note: Pick up financial, academic, or emotional problems, or general family problems by using the prompter: *Could you tell me more about that?*)

7. *Have you and your husband discussed the kind of college your child should go to?* (Use prompter: *Could you tell me more about that?*)

   a. *Is there any particular college you would like him to attend?*

   b. *How does your child feel about this?*

   c. *How did you choose this college?*

8. *Have you had anything to do with planning your child's high school program?*

   a. (If "yes" then:) *In what way?*

   b. *What sorts of requirements does he have to meet for college entrance?* (If respondent turns question back to interviewer, as far as interviewer knows such requirements may vary from college to college, and this is something interviewer is interested in studying.)

   c. *Have you talked with anyone about college requirements?*

   d. *With whom did you talk?*

   e. *What did they tell you?*

9. *Did you attend the meeting at Lakeshore High School held for parents of entering freshmen last February?*

   a. (If "yes" ask:) *We heard there was a meeting which we could not attend. Could you tell me about it?*

10. *Is there anything about your child's plans for the future that we have not discussed which you think is important for our study?*

11. *In closing, could you tell me something about the following:*
    a. *Your husband's occupation.*
    b. *Your husband's father's occupation.*
    c. *Your father's occupation.*
    d. *Are you employed at the present time? If so, what is your occupation?*
    e. *The number of years of schooling completed by your husband.*
    f. *The number of years of schooling completed by you.*
    g. *If college was attended by either wife or husband or both, which college?*

       Husband: Wife:

STUDENT SAMPLE

Let me tell you briefly what this interview is about. This is not an examination and it has nothing to do with your standing in school. We drew names at random from the class roll and that's how you have come to be included in our study. Anything that you say in this interview will be treated as confidential. No one here at school, or your friends or your parents, will hear about anything that you or I say here.

In this interview, we're interested in the future plans of high school students, and how decisions about those plans are made. We are interviewing parents, students, and school officials so as to find out as much as possible about how students plan for the future. In our interview with you we are particularly interested in your views about this matter.

Before we begin our interview, do you have any questions?

1. First we'd like to know a little about your work in junior high school.
    a. *How did you get along in junior high school?*
    b. (Whatever the response to *a*, ask:) *How do you mean?*
    c. *How did your parents feel you did in junior high school?*
    d. (Whatever the response to *c*, ask:) *How do you mean?*
    e. (If grades not mentioned by student, then ask:) *What kind of grades did you get in junior high school?*
    f. *How did your parents feel about the grades you got?*
    g. *How do you mean?*
    h. *How did you feel about your grades?*
    i. *How do you mean?*
    j. *How did your friends feel about the grades you got?*
    k. *How do you mean?*
    l. *What kind of grades did your friends get?*
2. I understand your first report card was sent home the other day.
    a. *What was the first thing that happened after your card was delivered?*

b. *What happened then?* (This should be repeated for as long as necessary.)

c. (If, after exhausting this line of questioning, the parents' discussion of the report card is not mentioned, ask:) *Did your parents discuss the card with you?*

d. *How did they feel about your grades?*

e. *What did they say?*

f. *Do things always happen like that when you get a report card?* (Make sure you pick up "unusual" occurrences, circumstances, interpretations, etc.)

g. (If friends are not mentioned in response to questions above, ask:) *Did you discuss your card with your friends?*

h. *What did they say?*

3. *How did you go about planning your high school program?* (Pause.)

a. *What was the first thing that happened?*

b. *What happened next?* (This line of questioning should continue until information is exhausted.)

c. (If parents are not mentioned, ask:) *Did you talk it over with your parents?*

d. *What did you talk about?*

e. *Then what happened?* (Exhaust this line of questioning.)

f. (If friends are not mentioned ask:) *Did you talk to your friends about it?*

g. *What did they say?*

h. (Refer to the form, then ask:) *I see that you had to choose between Plan I and Plan II. What plan did you choose?*

i. *Does it make any difference what plan you choose?*

j. *How do you mean?*

4. a. *Did you talk with anyone at school about your program?*

b. *Who did you talk to?*

c. *What did he (she) say about your program?*

5. (For those who have chosen Plan I, ask:) *What sorts of entrance requirements do you have to meet to get into college?*

a. *Have you talked to anyone about college requirements?*

b. *Who did you talk to?*

c. *What did he (she, they) tell you?*

6. *What do you think you would like to do after leaving high school?*

a. (If college is mentioned then go on to *b*. If not, ask:) *What do you think you would like to do immediately after leaving high school?*

b. *How do you think your parents feel about that?* (Ask with respect to *career* plans and *college* plans.)

c. *Have you talked to your parents about your future plans?*

d. (If response to *c* is no, then ask:) *Why not?*

e. How do you mean?

f. (If the response to *c* is *yes*, then ask:) *When was the last time you talked with your parents about your future plans?*

g. What did you talk about? (Use prompters if necessary.)

7. (For students who don't plan to go to college ask:) *Was the possibility of your going to college ever considered?*

   a. Could you tell me more about that?

   b. How do you feel about that?

8. (For those who plan to go to college ask:) *Do you remember the first time that the subject of college was discussed at home?*

   a. How old were you then?

   b. When was the last time you talked to your parents about college plans?

   c. What did you talk about?

   d. Has there ever been any question about whether you would go to college?

   e. Could you tell me more about that?

9. *Have you and your parents discussed the kind of college you should go to?*

   a. Is there any particular college they would like you to attend?

   b. Why do you think they chose that college?

   c. How do you feel about the college they've chosen?

   d. Do you want to go to a particular college?

10. *How have things been going since school began?* (If only school situations are mentioned, then ask about situations outside of school, or vice versa.)

    a. Have you talked to anyone on the faculty since school started about anything connected with school?

    b. Who have you talked to?

    c. What did you talk about?

    d. What happened?

    e. If you had a problem in school who would you go to see about it?

    f. Have any of your friends had any school problems?

    g. Who did they see about it?

    h. What happened?

OUTSIDE COUNSELOR SAMPLE

1. *How many counselors are there in the counseling and guidance program in your school?*

2. *Are they full-time or part-time?* (If part-time, question 3.)

3. *How much time is devoted to counseling duties?*

   a. How did you get into counseling?

b. *Are there any special requirements at your school?*

c. *How do students come to your attention?* (different ways of entering the system)

d. *What kinds of students do you come into contact with from day to day?*

e. *Which kinds do you see the most?*

f. *Would you tell me about the most recent case that you had which was of this kind?* (In detail—especially kinds of things he does.)

g. *Who referred this student to you?*

h. *What did the student do that led to the referral?*

i. *What kinds of information did you have about the student before he came to see you?*

j. *What did you think was the problem?*

k. *How did you handle the problem?*

l. *Did you talk with anyone else at school about the case?*
   1. *Who were the persons? What do they do in school?*
   2. *What features were discussed?*
   3. *Did you talk with parents?*
   If no, ask question *m;* if yes, *n* and *o.*

m. *What did you do then?*

n. *What was the last thing you had to do with the case?*

o. *What was the last thing you heard about the case?*
   1. *From whom did you get the information?*

p. *Was any of the information about this case recorded anywhere?*
   1. *What was recorded and where?*

q. *Who has access to the information while the case is open or closed?*

COUNSELOR AND SOCIAL WORKER SCHEDULE FOR LAKESHORE HIGH

1. *Do you work full-time or part-time as a counselor?*
   Full-time_____ Part-time_____

2. (If part-time): *How much time do you devote to counseling duties?*
   a. *How did you get into counseling?*
   b. *Are there any special requirements for counselors at this school?*
   c. *What kinds of training do you think a counselor should have? How's that?*
   d. *How do students come to your attention?*
      1. *Is there any other way they might come to your attention?*
      2. *How's that?*
   e. *What kinds of students do you come into contact with from day to day?* (Prompter: *What are the reasons they come to your attention?*)
   f. *Which kinds of students do you see the most?*
   g. *What do you mean by X type (or X types) of student?*

h. *Would you tell me about the most recent case that you had that was of X type (or X types)?* (In detail, especially behavior of the student.)

i. *Who referred this student to you?*

j. *What did the student do that led to the referral?*

k. *What kinds of information did you have about the student before he came to see you? What was the source of the information?*

    1. *Did you collect any information about the student on your own?*

l. *What did you think was the problem?*

m. *How did you handle the problem?*

n. *Did you talk with anyone else here at school about the case?*
Yes_____ No_____

    1. *Who were the persons you talked with?* (For each person mentioned: *What is his position at school?*)

    2. *What did you talk with him about?*

o. *Did you talk with the student's parents about the case?* Yes_____ No_____ (If yes:) *What did you talk about?*

p. *What was the last thing you had to do with the case?*

q. *What was the last thing you heard about the case?*

    1. *From whom did you get the information?*

r. *Is it customary for him (them) to notify you about the closing of a case?*

s. *How do you keep track of the information that you get when you're handling a case?*

    1. *Are there any formal records made of the information?* Yes_____ No_____ (If yes:) *What kind of thing do you record?*

    2. *How are these records filed?*

    3. *Are these files shared among the counselors?* Yes_____ No _____ (If yes:) *Can you give me an example of such an occasion?*

    4. *Do any of the other school personnel have occasion to refer to the files while the case is active or after it is closed?* Yes _____ No _____ (If yes:) *Can you give me an example of such an occasion?*

    5. *Are there any other school personnel who might have occasion to refer to the files?*

INDEX